Encounter Jesus

From Discovery to Discipleship

FR. DAVE PIVONKA, T.O.R.,
and
DEACON RALPII POYO

servant
AN IMPRINT OF
FRANCISCAN MEDIA
Cincinnati, Ohio

Scripture texts in this work are taken from the *New American Bible, revised edition* © 2010, 1991, 1986, 1970 Confraternity of Christian Doctrine, Washington, D.C., and are used by permission of the copyright owner. All Rights Reserved. No part of the *New American Bible* may be reproduced in any form without permission in writing from the copyright owner. Quotes are taken from the English translation of the *Catechism of the Catholic Church* for the United States of America (indicated as *CCC*), 2nd ed. Copyright 1997 by United States Catholic Conference—Libreria Editrice Vaticana.

LIBRARY OF CONGRESS CATALOGING-IN-PUBLICATION DATA
Pivonka, Dave.
Encounter Jesus : from discovery to discipleship / Dave Pivonka, T.O.R., and Deacon Ralph Poyo.
pages cm
Includes bibliographical references.
ISBN 978-1-61636-789-3 (alk. paper)
1. Christian life—Catholic authors. 2. Jesus Christ. 3. Bible. Gospels— Criticism, interpretation, etc. I. Title.
BX2350.3.P5645 2014
248.4—dc23

ISBN 978-1-61636-789-3

Copyright ©2014, Dave Pivonka and Ralph Poyo. All rights reserved.

Published by Servant Books, an imprint of Franciscan Media.
28 W. Liberty St.
Cincinnati, OH 45202
www.FranciscanMedia.org

Printed in the United States of America.
Printed on acid-free paper.
17 18   5 4 3

CONTENTS

⚜Every book has a story, and this one is no different.

Deacon Ralph is a permanent deacon, married for over twenty-five years, with five beautiful daughters. Fr. Dave has been a Franciscan priest for about eighteen years and lives with four friars who, while maybe not quite as beautiful as Ralph's daughters, are blessings in his life.

While the paths that brought us to write this book have been different, our passions are very similar. We both want everyone to come to know the lifesaving love of Jesus Christ. You see, we have a heart for evangelization and discipleship, and we love sharing the message of God's love. It has been a primary focus of our lives for quite some time. Presently the Lord has both of us traveling all over the United States and the world preaching God's love and mercy.

On one occasion we were comparing notes about our ministry and were surprised by our similar experiences. We both find that traveling is often a chore and a blessing. For example, it drives us both crazy when the guy sitting in front of us on the airplane tries to get his suitcase, which is the size of a twin mattress, into the overhead bin. Really?

Another similar and certainly much more important experience is that many people are encountering the living God through our ministries. People's lives are being changed. God is doing a great work and is allowing us to be intimately involved in the New Evangelization. We are blessed to see the lives of men and women being transformed from their encounter of God.

The more we talked, the more we realized that we often hear the same types of stories and comments:

"God is real! I have never experienced him before now. This is amazing."

"My wife and I go to church every week but felt something was missing. We felt like there was something more. I think we found it."

"God loves me! He doesn't just love the world or everyone—*he loves me*. I have experienced this for the first time."

It seems that often when people have an experience of God, they know that something has to change. They know that if they are going to take their faith life more seriously, they have to do some things differently. "Where do I go from here?" and "How can I keep this alive?" are very familiar questions to us. We think that what people are really trying to get at is: "How does one become a disciple of Jesus? What does one have to do in order to continue to encounter God?"

We usually deal with men and women who have been Catholic most of their lives. Now, having had a personal encounter with Christ, they feel ill-equipped to move forward in their faith. They are stuck and not sure what to do.

There are, of course, some things that all Christians ought to do if they are serious about growing in their relationship with Christ. Things like prayer, developing a rich sacramental life, detachment from the world, recognizing the enemy, discipleship, evangelization, and living in the Spirit are all key elements in the spiritual life. In this book we deal with these issues and others. Our hope is that the reader will be able to benefit from our experiences and use this book as a tool for growth in their relationship with Christ and his Church.

We spent time in prayer and reflection to discern what we should address in this book and who should deal with what topic. We identified each chapter's author, though some of the stories make it pretty obvious. (Fr. Dave rarely, if ever, speaks of his wife, and Deacon Ralph does not hear confessions!)

It is our hope that this book will help you in your journey with the Lord. Be assured of our prayers for you as you continue to seek God and his plan for your life. May you be drawn ever more into the glorious life of our Savior.

—*Fr. Dave and Deacon Ralph*

CHAPTER ONE

The Encounter
• *Fr. Dave* •

Jesus sat down and taught the crowds from the boat. After he had finished speaking, he said to Simon, "Put out into deep water and lower your nets for a catch." Simon said in reply, "Master, we have worked hard all night and have caught nothing, but at your command I will lower the nets." When they had done this, they caught a great number of fish and their nets were tearing. They signaled to their partners in the other boat to come to help them. They came and filled both boats so that they were in danger of sinking. When Simon Peter saw this, he fell at the knees of Jesus and said, "Depart from me, Lord, for I am a sinful man...."

Jesus said to Simon, "Do not be afraid; from now on you will be catching men." When they brought their boats to the shore, they left everything and followed him. (Luke 5:3–8, 10–11)

It all begins with an encounter.

Peter was probably tired and frustrated and wanted to go home. It had been a long, unproductive night. Catching no fish makes for a bad night and often leads to a grouchy fisherman. But his work was not quite finished. He was completing the difficult task of washing and mending his fishing nets.

Maybe he had heard of Jesus, but probably not. Jesus wasn't that well-known yet. However, on this particular day, Peter had to notice the commotion and the crowd around Jesus. "Who is this guy, and what do they want from him?"

Suddenly Peter noticed Jesus getting into his boat. "Whoa, wait a minute."

"Take me out a little ways from the crowd," stated Jesus.

"Really? I'm a fisherman, not a taxi service. All I want to do is wash my nets and go home."

Jesus could be rather persuasive, so Peter took him away from the shore, and Jesus continued to preach. When he was finished he suggested the men fish.

We don't know exactly what Jesus said to the crowds, but it became evident to Peter that there was something different about this man. "Master, we are tired, we've been doing this all night, but I will do as you wish." Do as he wishes—always a good idea.

Wow, this Jesus could fish too. Peter was amazed at the catch. He did something remarkable: There in that boat full of flailing fish, he fell to his knees and said, "Leave me, Lord; I'm a sinful man."

Is that odd? They pulled in a bunch of fish, and Peter was struck by his sinfulness. Where did that come from? Had Jesus been preaching on sin? Maybe. Or perhaps Peter was so struck by the amazing catch of fish that he became aware that there had to be something else at work. Jesus had to have something more than good fishing instinct. In Jesus there was something special, something different, maybe something divine.

What we know for certain is that Peter was overwhelmed with a sense of his sin. He was repentant and frightened. Oh, and his life would forever change.

"Don't be afraid, Peter, from now on you will be catching men."

With no questions to clarify and no hesitation, Peter left everything (his circle of friends, his livelihood, his native land) and followed Jesus.

This was an encounter that Peter surely was not prepared for and one that forever changed his life. And if we think about it, it can change our lives as well.

An Essential Encounter

Everyone has significant encounters that have profound impact on the course of their lives. Some encounters may in fact change the very direction of our lives. We have encounters that affect decisions about where we go to college, what career we pursue, whom we marry. Some of the encounters seem insignificant at first; only later do we come to understand how important they were. The importance of other encounters is evident at the moment of their happening.

Our spiritual life begins a new path with a personal encounter with Jesus Christ. This personal encounter is essential in our spiritual life. Pope Francis addressed this beautifully in an Advent message: He said that we are on a pilgrimage of faith "to encounter the Lord and, most of all, to allow ourselves to be encountered by him..... We must allow ourselves to be encountered by him...to allow him to enter us. It is he who makes all new.... Christ renews the heart, the soul, life, hope."[1]

Pope Francis also declared in his apostolic exhortation *Evangelii Gaudium*:

The joy of the gospel fills the hearts and lives of all who encounter Jesus....

I invite all Christians, everywhere, at this very moment, to a renewed personal encounter with Jesus Christ.[2]

Our life radically changes when we have an encounter in which God becomes personal—not just a force, power, or judge, but a loving, personal God. Such encounters are eternally important. I remember one such encounter.

One Starry Night

I was a very young boy, and my family was attending a retreat in a small town in New Mexico. One evening everyone gathered around a large bonfire, and we sang songs, prayed, and had a wonderful time.

For little boys campfires are magical. I was enthralled watching the embers drift up into the darkness, mingling with and ultimately getting lost in the stars. Dismissing my mother's continued cautioning, I inched closer and closer to the flames. I guess the goal was to get as close to the fire as possible without actually combusting.

I can't fully explain it, but at that moment I felt extremely small in the midst of everything. The outdoors, the fire, the stars, the universe: It was all so big, and I was so small. I had a wonderful feeling of God's bigness in the middle of my being, of being overwhelmed by the majesty of God. At the same time I knew that I was special to Jesus, that I mattered to him, and that he was close to me.

Big stuff for a little kid. God was out there but was also close. I could feel his presence and his love for me. Perhaps in my heart or soul I could feel his fire. It was an encounter of grace, an encounter with a very big, personal God.

Have you had an encounter of grace? It's really important that each of us does. Many people who have not had such encounters describe their journey of faith as a fairly nondescript course, void of significant markers. They speak of faith in lifeless, bland, impersonal terms.

When individuals describe intimate experiences of God, they use words like *life-changing, new, powerful,* and *transforming.* There is excitement and exuberance in their recountings of their stories. They are able to share events in their spiritual lives that impacted them and brought about new purpose and hope. I think we all need such markers by which we can give witness to God's work in our lives.

It may be that you have not had such an encounter. Your spiritual life may be much like that of someone lost in the desert, not knowing where you are going or where you have been. It may be that you don't have significant events to look to, encounters that would spur you on in your walk with God. There may be lots of reasons why this is the case. What is important to remember is, don't despair.

God is alive and is on the move. He is touching hearts every day, at every moment of the day, and he desires to make himself known to each of us, his children. Much of this book is about making ourselves available to see God's presence. He is there; we often miss him.

I invite you to ask God to break into your world and show you that he is present. Ask Christ to reveal himself and make himself known. The Lord desires that you encounter him. "Knock and the door will be opened to you" (Matthew 7:7).

Encounters of the Daily Kind
St. Peter had an initial encounter with Jesus on the shores of the Sea of Galilee, but there would certainly be others. This is true for us as well. While we may have had an initial encounter with God, he wants us to continue to experience him. It's important that we continue to encounter Christ through graced moments in our daily lives.

In an initial encounter with Jesus, a seed is planted. But if we are not intentional in seeing that the seed is watered, the grace of the encounter shrivels away. The encounter with God becomes a sentimental story, a relic of the past rather than a life-changing and life-giving experience. Fortunately, Christ is ever present to us and desires to make himself known. He is always ready to encounter us again.

One of the gifts that many of the saints had was the awareness of God's presence. They were able to see him in all situations—in abundance or in scarcity, in the light or in the dark. The saints are able to see God. God is there. This is, I believe, a secret to holiness.

To be aware of his presence usually requires a change in us. God does not seem to be where we want him to be, but often we fail to see him where he is. As we grow closer to God, we are able to experience him in the beauty of a sunset, the giggle of a child, or even the loneliness of the elderly. God is there; are we seeing him?

One of the best ways to grow in the spiritual life is to move from an occasional, fleeting experience of God to consistent encounters. This allows the narrative of one's spiritual life to move from "I remember an experience of God when I was young" to "Let me tell you what happened this morning."

There are two simple things that will help you be able see the Lord. First, pray with expectant faith. Ask God to show himself, and expect him to show himself. "God, I want to see you today!"

I don't believe that God wants to be a stranger to us. I think God wants to be a constant companion, and we should pray that way. We should ask God to be close to us and fully expect that he will be near. That doesn't mean that our spiritual life will become a 24/7 spiritual high, but in time we will see that God is more present to us than we ever realized.

Second, look for him. "Lord, I am going to look for you today. Reveal yourself to me. Whether it be in my prayer, in a friend, or in line at the market, just let me see you." No doubt God is there. Sure, sometimes he is hidden in the disguise of the poor, a neighbor, or a cranky colleague, but he is there. He is always there.

God desires that we encounter him not once but continually. The world is graced, and the Lord is present; those with eyes of faith are able to see.

An encounter with God opens a whole new world for us. It is a world of hope in the midst of chaos, a universe in which the power of mercy overwhelms guilt and despair. It is an existence in which God is fully alive, and so are we. Such is the grace of an encounter with the living God.

Invitation to Faith

• Deacon Ralph •

When he entered Capernaum, a centurion approached him and appealed to him, saying, "Lord, my servant is lying at home paralyzed, suffering dreadfully." He said to him, "I will come and cure him." The centurion said in reply, "Lord, I am not worthy to have you enter under my roof; only say the word and my servant will be healed...."

And Jesus said to the centurion, "You may go; as you have believed, let it be done for you." And at that very hour [his] servant was healed. (Matthew 8:5–8, 13)

By the time Jesus walked through Capernaum, the crowds already had a pulse on him and his ministry. The villagers were marveling about this new prophet who had the power to heal people. The streets were filled with stories heard from trusted friends and family. Everyone, Roman and Jew, was privy to the scoop on this man.

The centurion was no exception. Perhaps he had witnessed Jesus healing someone, heard him teach with great authority, or learned about such events from a trusted friend. His love and desperation led him to reach out to Jesus, with the hope that Jesus would help him. One can infer that he had a clear understanding of who Jesus was.

Once Jesus agreed to help, the centurion was certain that his servant would be healed. In fact, he did not even need the added assurance of witnessing Jesus touch the servant or speak to him. If Jesus wanted the man healed, he would be healed. Nothing else was needed but to hear Jesus proclaim, "Go, let it be done for you according to your faith." Upon hearing those words, the centurion left. This was an act of faith.

Faith Is Trusting

Bishop Fulton Sheen defined faith as "the acceptance of truth on the authority of God who reveals it."[3] All truth comes from God, and the invitation of faith is to accept truth.

Before Adam and Eve sinned in the Garden of Eden, the devil first led them to doubt the word of God. The serpent tricked Eve into questioning whether God's intention was for good or simply to prevent her from becoming like him (see Genesis 3:4–5). Adam and Eve lost their faith in God and in his promise. Therefore they disobeyed his command, and from that point on, the inclination of humanity has been to doubt God's word.

Doubt leads to separation from God. Humanity wandered from its creator and fell into greater and frequent sin. God did not turn away from humanity but was always at work to bring people to himself. God had a plan; God always has a plan.

In contrast to the unfaithfulness of Adam, Abraham was an honorable man whose faithfulness made him well respected. Through Abraham and his descendants would come a people who trusted in God. But this trust had to be established. After promising to make Abraham the father of many descendants, God asked Abraham to go to a new land. Trusting in God's word, Abraham packed up his family and left.

As Abraham grew to respect and fear God, he experienced God's blessing. Abraham's son Isaac witnessed his father's ardent love, trust, and obedience to God. These characteristics provided him the model and instruction needed to grow in faith. Isaac came to know and trust in his father's God. He in turn passed on this intimate faith and knowledge to his sons, Jacob and Esau. Jacob passed on his grandfather's faith to his twelve sons, who became the patriarchs of the twelve tribes of Israel.

As Abraham's family grew into the nation of Israel, they were all united with one common thread: knowledge and faith in God! Therefore Abraham is known as the father of faith (see Romans 4:16–24). He heard the word of God, believed it to be true, and acted upon it.

Many people believe that faith is merely knowledge of God, but knowledge of God is only the beginning of a faith journey. The journey toward a deeper faith in God is a journey toward deeper trust. What is the value of knowing about God if this knowledge doesn't lead you to trust in him?

St. Peter was traveling across the sea with the apostles when Jesus came toward the boat, walking on the water. As Peter witnessed this miracle, he asked the Lord if he could join him. "'Lord, if it is you, command me to come to you on the water.' He said, 'Come.' Peter got out of the boat and began to walk on the water toward Jesus" (Matthew 14:28–29).

Peter was certainly taking a risk to step out of the comfort of the vessel he traveled in with his friends. With his eyes on the Lord, he stepped out of the boat, believing that Jesus was calling him for a specific reason.

Like Peter, we are being called out of the security of our worldly boats into the waters of Jesus's life. As we grow in discipleship, the Lord will repeatedly call us to trust in his ability to handle every part of our lives.

Fathoming Faith

I remember an occasion when I had to trust the Lord. I was reading Matthew 6:33, "But seek first the kingdom of God and his righteousness, and all these things will be given you besides." I recognized that God was making a promise to me. If I sought the kingdom of God first, above all else in my life, he was going to take care of all my needs. The phrase "these things" means food, clothing, shelter, and all the rest of my needs.

Did God really mean that? Could I really trust him to provide for everything in my life?

This reminded me of Abraham and his model as father of faith. As I stated earlier, Abraham is known as the father of faith because he heard the word of God, believed it to be true, and acted upon it. If the promise God was making to me was true, then I needed to act upon it.

This required me to carve out time from my busy life, to make time to strive for the kingdom of God. What would that look like? I began to set aside time every morning for prayer and Scripture study.

This was a difficult task at first, because I desired instant gratification. I was used to getting what I wanted when I wanted it. I expected to experience the amazing movement of God every time I prayed. That did not happen.

After a few days of prayer, I was frustrated because I had not experienced any powerful movement of God. My prayer was not an exciting rush of emotions but rather a struggle and a grind. I felt empty and questioned if God was even with me.

Then I realized that perhaps this struggle and emotional wrestling had a purpose. Perhaps God had a lesson for me to learn from this. Was it possible I was seeking a feeling rather than seeking the person of God? I have a tendency to make everything about how I feel. Can we make our faith only about feeling?

We can answer this most profoundly when we look at what Jesus did on the cross. I am sure he did not feel like getting crucified, but he did it out of love for me. His death was not merely a random act of violence but an act of love. Authentic love is not only a feeling but most importantly a choice; it is sacrificial.

Another discovery was that God really could take care of my needs. I experienced this in his provision of time. At what I sensed was God's request, I carved out thirty minutes for prayer a day, even though I did not believe I had the time. What I experienced was a miraculous multiplication of time. Each day that I took time to pray, I was able to accomplish everything that needed to be done.

I was also more patient and loving on those days I prayed. God was faithful. He really did take care of me.

Transforming Faith

As I grew in my faith, I realized I was changing. It is a fundamental truth that the Gospel has the power to transform. How, you ask? A great question.

When we come to believe that Jesus is real, we act on that faith. We strive to live as Jesus lived. What he desires for our lives takes on new importance. We want to please him with our words and actions. This is a process of conversion that takes time and patience.

It is also something we need help with; we cannot do it alone. Jesus chose to gather men and women into a community of which he was the center. He knew that we need people who are walking this journey of faith to help guide us. Like the coals of a fire gathered around the heat source, each member contributes to another's growth.

We are also given the Holy Spirit as a helper. He will lead us into a fuller life with God. As I grew in faith, I experienced a strong sense of the presence of God's love, joy, and peace. I later came to understand that these were some of the fruits one receives when living with and in the Spirit (see Galatians 5:22–23). I also had a hunger for God's Word and a desire to spend time with him.

On the other hand, I noticed God's absence in my heart when I returned to some of my sinful habits. I felt that God had left me. One day I asked, "God, where are you? Where did you go?" God gently replied, "It is no longer acceptable for you to give yourself to sin and still experience my presence." His loving conviction called me to repentance and reconciliation.

I could not see what was happening at the time. Now I understand that I was gaining intimate knowledge of my Lord Jesus Christ through the action of the Holy Spirit. My heart was being drawn to God.

It is generally true that we only trust those whom we know. So we must know God in order to fully trust in him. This was the experience of the centurion who approached Jesus and asked him to heal his servant. He had learned about Jesus and knew with great certainty that Jesus was someone who could and would help. Once he believed this truth, he acted on it. Jesus generously granted the desire of his heart. His servant was healed.

Imagine what would have happened had the centurion not believed. He would never have asked for healing, and his servant would have probably died. This is a profound truth of faith: When we believe that Jesus is who he says he is, we must act on that belief. Then our life will be changed forever!

Real Faith

Faith is not faith until it is all-encompassing. We cannot hold anything back.

I was leading a youth leadership training day in the mountains of North Carolina for a group of teens when this truth came alive. We woke up early, and I gave a teaching on deepening our faith in God. After the teaching, we set out to rappel a 150-foot rock cliff.

We worked our way to the top of the cliff via a trail around the side of the mountain. Once on top, another leader and I instructed the teens on the equipment we would be using. We also taught them procedures to ensure their safety.

After about an hour of questions, the first student was ready to rappel down the cliff. We connected one end of the rope to a tree, while the other end dangled over the cliff. I was attached to my own safety line, in order to help the students over the edge of the cliff and to provide reassurance. They knew they could trust me, or so I thought.

When Matthew was ready, I asked him if he had any last questions, and he stated that he did not. I then instructed him to weight the rope. This meant that Matthew should tighten his body so that it was like a tree trunk and then lean back over the cliff. This was the most difficult task of rappelling, because it demanded trust in the equipment and trust in me.

Matthew began. But instead of leaning back, he kept his weight on top of the cliff and simply squatted, as if he were doing deep knee bends.

"What are you doing?" I asked.

"Leaning back," he responded.

"No, you're not; look at the way you're standing. Where is your weight?"

Matthew did a quick assessment and realized he was not weighting the rope.

I then asked, "Why are you doing that?"

"I'm afraid the rope won't hold me," he said

In a firm tone I called out his name: "Matthew." His fearful eyes looked to me, and I said, "The only way you will trust the rope is to place your weight on it. You need to lean back over the edge of the cliff."

Slowly, somewhat hesitantly, Matthew leaned back, trusting the rope and me, and began to work his way down the cliff. Once he realized that the rope would hold him, he was totally free to enjoy the thrill of rappelling down a 150-foot cliff. He bounced around the face of it, smiling from ear to ear. As soon as he finished, he wanted to rappel off the cliff again. Matthew had learned to trust the rope and to trust me.

I have had similar experiences when learning to trust God. God can hold me. But until I place myself in a position of total trust in him, I will not know that he can hold me.

Leaning off the cliff for me was trusting God with my finances. The Lord had convicted my wife and me that we did not trust him. At the beginning of each month, we would pay our bills, and if we had any money left, we would give it to God. Surrendering our finances seemed like the biggest challenge in our journey to trust God.

However, God was inviting us to trust the rope, to give him control. So Susan and I decided that every month the first check we would write would be our tithe check to God. There have been months when the finances were very tight, but we have never been unable to meet our financial responsibilities. God has never let us down, and he never will. I would not have believed that before I weighted my financial rope!

As we learn to trust God, he will lead each of us to different cliffs and ask us to trust in him. Each of us is called to trust in areas of our lives specific to our journeys. For some, surrendering our children to the Lord is the greatest challenge. For others it may be their marriage or perhaps their future or their health.

Are you willing to place your faith in God in every area of your life? Will you give him everything? As Matthew experienced great joy when he finally let go and trusted, so too will you experience peace and joy when you trust the Lord with everything.

CHAPTER THREE

Freedom from Sin
• Fr. Dave •

They came bringing to him a paralytic carried by four men. Unable to get near Jesus because of the crowd, they opened up the roof above him. After they had broken through, they let down the mat on which the paralytic was lying. When Jesus saw their faith, he said to the paralytic, "Child, your sins are forgiven." (Mark 2:3–5)

I can only imagine the conversation between the paralytic and his friends:

> Friend #1: "Hmm, looks kind of busy; we are never going to be able to get to Jesus."
> Friend #2: "Well, I have a great idea…"
> Friend #3: "Splendid!"
> Friend #4: "It just might work."
> Paralytic: "I'll wait. No real hurry here, it's not like I am going anywhere."
> Jesus: "Your sins are forgiven."

I wonder if this is what the paralytic expected to receive from Jesus. Maybe this was more than he could have imagined. Being healed of paralysis is one thing, but having your sins forgiven—experiencing salvation—well, that's something altogether different, much more impressive. Probably not what he expected when he encountered Jesus that day.

It's Personal

We live in a world that is becoming less and less personal. We do many things alone today that once involved human interactions. An individual is able to take care of most banking needs without ever stepping into a bank and, more importantly, without ever speaking to another person. Social media has created a world of friends among individuals who have never actually met. By that I mean that they have never been in the same room, never shaken hands, never spoken to one another face-to-face. This has given rise to an entirely new etiquette (netiquette) for how people are to relate with each other.

One would think common sense would dictate that highly personal information should not be posted on one's Facebook page, but this is news for some. It seems obvious that a breakup with a girlfriend or boyfriend should not be done through a text message, but apparently not. Personal face-to-face encounters are becoming less common.

All this is to say that our world is becoming less personal and less relational. This has impacted our relationship with God and our relationships with one another.

Lots of people already have a hard time experiencing God as personal, and our current culture makes this even more difficult. Whether they are aware of it or not, many people see God as some power out there that does not have any real contact with them. There is little or no sense that God is personal with his people. This is perhaps most clearly seen in sin.

Sin isn't exactly a popular topic; however, it needs to be addressed.

Don't get me wrong, I don't get a kick out of talking about sin. It's just that a lack of honest discussion about the topic leaves many people confused and leads them astray. They cannot experience freedom over sin if they refuse to look at it, discuss it, and then conquer it.

A director of religious education once vented this frustration to me. Some of his colleagues, and sadly even some priests whom he knew, taught that the whole idea of sin was antiquated. He lamented, "We are not doing them (the people of God) any favors by not talking about sin."

Perhaps in an attempt to not make anyone feel bad or judged or offended, the issue of sin is rarely broached. It's kind of odd: We are a church that outsiders accuse of being obsessed with sin, but the reality is that we don't deal with the topic that much. Sure, we sin, but we don't dare talk about it and its consequences.

Obviously this is problematic on many levels. By not addressing sin in a straightforward manner, we never really deal with it. Our sin lives in the shadows and doesn't get exposed to the light of God's transforming power. God desires us to be radically holy; he wants you and me to be saints. But if we continue to shackle ourselves to sin, his plan for our growth is thwarted.

Let's Talk about Sin

First off, most people don't see sin as personal, but sin is always personal. When I sin I damage a relationship. I don't just break a rule; I break a bond. I break my relationship with God, who is passionately in love with me. How badly the relationship is broken depends on how serious the sin is. Mortal sin inflicts a deadly break, while venial offenses wound my relationship with God.

Imagine a spouse who has been unfaithful. He or she hasn't merely broken some rule or regulation imposed by a marriage license. Rather, hasn't one deeply offended and violated the trust of the beloved? Isn't the offense more than just breaking a law? Isn't it a rupture in the very nature of the relationship between the man and woman who have vowed to be faithful?

And doesn't this offense affect more than the spouses? Doesn't it affect the children, the extended family, and even friends? Clearly, the infidelity is more than a broken rule. It is personal.

And so it is with our sin and God. When I choose sin, I am not merely breaking a rule, a law, or a commandment. I am fracturing a relationship with God, whose love is deeply personal.

Often people come to me in confession and say that they know they are sinners but just don't know what their sins are. I can appreciate that, and it's good they are at confession. But we need to know our sins!

I need to know how I sin, and I need to be specific. Only then can I really repent for that sin and begin to experience victory.

The Church clearly identifies some things as sinful. God gave us the Ten Commandments, by which we are to love him and love one another (see Exodus 20). Jesus confirmed these and added new demands (see Matthew 5:18–38); he also gave us the Beatitudes (Matthew 5:1–11). In addition, the Church offers six precepts for our guidance (see *CCC* 2041–2043, 2048). These enable us to live fully in the light of the Gospel and to love the way Jesus loved us.

Sometimes it's difficult to see areas of sin in our lives. I might have a log in my eye that keeps me from seeing reality (see Matthew 7:4). Or I might have a sin of pride that masks itself as something nobler.

It's essential that we present ourselves to God and ask him to show us our sin. I always begin confession, "Come, Holy Spirit, and show us our sin, so that we may know your mercy." I am quite certain that if one faithfully goes before God in prayer and asks him to reveal sin, God will grant that prayer. If we truly want to change and root out sin, God will help us. God wants us to know our sin more than we want to know it, so ask for his help.

Close Encounters

At the end of John's Gospel, Jesus appeared to the apostles in order to give them one last instruction before ascending to heaven. This would be their last encounter with Jesus, and he wanted them to be clear about his grace being available to all people. Jesus told his disciples, "Whose sins you forgive are forgiven" (John 20:23).

Jesus's death and resurrection unleashed the torrents of the Father's mercy, which will forever be available to all who seek it. Thus humanity can be free from the tyranny of sin and death. True conversion is possible and necessary if we are to be disciples of Jesus. This life-changing grace of conversion is powerfully experienced in the sacrament of reconciliation.

The *Catechism* speaks of the sacrament of reconciliation as "the sacrament of conversion" (*CCC* 1423). In this sacrament the door is flung open for an encounter with Christ. An individual approaches God seeking mercy, and a priest is waiting to open the floodgates of this stream of grace.

There is no way to fully explain the gift I have in being able to hear confessions. I think most priests have had the same experience. I recall a conversation with a fellow friar who was having a particularly difficult time in his life and ministry. The topic of confession came up. "It has saved my life," he shared. "Being able to hear confession, it saved my life; it kept me sane."

This priest told me that in the midst of personal difficulty, hearing confessions was the one thing to which he looked forward to. He was able to be Jesus to the penitents, and quite wonderfully the penitents were able to be Jesus to him. The sacrament was a personal encounter for both the priest and each penitent. This is one of the many reasons the Church won't allow confession over the phone or the Internet. Personal encounters are graced.

Finally, I am reminded of what Pope Francis wrote to priests in *Evangelii Gaudium:*

> I want to remind priests that the confessional must not be a torture chamber but rather an encounter with the Lord's mercy which spurs us on to do our best. (44)

I am aware oftentimes that people are nervous about coming to me and confessing their sins. I understand this nervousness, because I have been there. I go to confession on a regular basis, and I know how it feels to be a little nervous. I know what it is to wait in line thinking, "Not again." I too wonder what the priest is going to think.

When you approach me (or any priest) to go to confession, keep in mind that I too am a sinner. You are not approaching someone terribly different from yourself. Both priest and penitent are in need of God's mercy. Yes, I know what it is to be desperately in need of the mercy of God.

I am reminded of this whenever a penitent comes to me in confession. I know that I will soon be in the confession line, seeking the very same mercy of God. I hope this dictates how I receive the penitent and perhaps how penitents come to me.

Another concern I often hear is "What will the priest think?" To be honest, we don't think a lot. Wait, that didn't come out right. What I mean is that I don't spend a lot of time dwelling on what you have done. This may sound odd, but what you have done is not as important to me as what you are doing. You are coming before the Lord, admitting your sin, desiring to change, and seeking the Lord's forgiveness. That is what I think about, so don't worry.

How great is it that in confession both the priest and the penitent are able to encounter Jesus together? What a beautifully intimate experience of God's love.

Christ in the Struggle

It is also important that we not allow ourselves to despair over our sin. Sin is a part of our human struggle. The Scriptures remind us that all have sinned and fallen short (see Roman 3:32). The fact that I have sinned does not mean that I can't be holy. All saints sinned (of course, with the notable exception of Our Lady). Sin is one of the few things that all saints have in common. We become holy by working through our sinfulness, not by ignoring it.

While it is true that I sin, it is equally true that God will never abandon me. God is in the midst of my darkness. He sees me, and he loves me. Some of the most beautiful moments of grace for me are when I "go to my Father" to experience his loving embrace (Luke 15:18).

God is all-loving and all-forgiving. There are no qualifications to this and no exceptions. God is love, and sin is a turning away, a running from God's life-giving love. Having a clear understanding of sin is essential to encountering God and his mercy. God's forgiveness is another marvelous expression of his great love for us.

St. Paul says that all things work for the glory of God (see Romans 8:28). While it is sometimes difficult to see, Christ is also present in our struggles with sin. God is always with us, and this is true in times of temptation and even in our occasional fall. He does not abandon us and then wait for us to return to him in the sacrament. If we allow him, God can use our sin to draw us to himself. Our fallen flesh wants to accuse and shame us when we sin, but Christ wants to encourage and draw us to himself. When we fall there is often a moment of grace in which we come to know our helplessness and our need for God.

Our human tendency is to believe that we are invincible and that we may not need God. Sin invites us to face our weakness, and this has the possibility of drawing us to Jesus. We come to realize we are helpless and need God's grace. Perhaps this is what Paul was speaking of when he said that he boasts of his weakness (see 2 Corinthians 11:30). Falling can keep us humble.

The prodigal son was forced to confront his sin. After "coming to his senses," he returned to his father's house. As we know, his father was waiting for him and threw a party to welcome his son home. It's important to note that the elder brother did not enter into the celebration. He was not aware of his sin and did not know his need for the father (see Luke 15:11–32).

I can't live this life without the help of God's grace. Left to my own power, I will continue to fail. My sin humbles me. When I recognize this, I perceive an invitation for me to return to God, the eternal source of mercy. My failure reminds me of my need for God.

Of course, this is never an excuse for sin, but it can be an example of bringing good from something bad. In the end I see this as a testament to God's power and grace. He has the ability to even use our sin and brokenness to bring us closer to him.

Jesus is inviting us to encounter him in his unending mercy and forgiveness. Let us always respond to this invitation of grace, that we may experience a close encounter of the best kind.

CHAPTER FOUR

Good-Bye, World

• *Deacon Ralph* •

On [Saul's] journey, as he was nearing Damascus, a light from the sky suddenly flashed around him. He fell to the ground and heard a voice saying to him, "Saul, Saul, why are you persecuting me?" He said, "Who are you, sir?" The reply came, "I am Jesus, whom you are persecuting. Now get up and go into the city and you will be told what you must do." (Acts 9:3–6)

⚜A new star of Judaism was rising from the ranks of the Pharisees. His name was Saul, and he was a well-educated, zealous protector of the Jewish faith. He had taken it upon himself to destroy a new threat to Judaism called Christianity.

On the road from Jerusalem to Damascus, Saul encountered Jesus. This confrontation left Saul both blinded by the light and confused by Jesus's verbal confrontation. In this condition he needed to be led into town by his companions.

For three days Saul denied himself both food and water in order to free himself for meditation on this event. He wrestled with the truth of Jesus's identity. Then one of Jesus's disciples, Ananias, came to Saul and restored his sight by laying hands on him. Ananias also offered to baptize Saul in the name of Jesus.

By agreeing to receive baptism, Saul made a very serious decision. He chose to leave all he had in order to give himself completely to Jesus. This conversion set Saul on the way to becoming the apostle you and I know as St. Paul.

Paul's path would no longer include the destruction of Christianity; in fact, he was going to follow Jesus. He would now pursue "the prize of God's upward calling, in Christ Jesus" (Philippians 3:14). He would consider his life prior to meeting Christ as lost or dead (see Philippians 3:8).

St. Paul came to recognize his baptism as the complete gift of himself to Jesus. He wrote to the church in Rome, "Are you unaware that we who were baptized into Christ Jesus were baptized into his death?" (Romans 6:3). The death was not literal, but it represented a complete donation of one's life to God. St. Paul chose to let go of everything in the world and make himself totally available to Jesus through the will of the Holy Spirit.

As baptism was the pivotal point in St. Paul's life, so it is for every individual. It is "a new birth to a living hope" (1 Peter 1:3). The *Catechism* tells us:

> Holy Baptism is the basis of the whole Christian life, the gateway to life in the Spirit…and the door which gives access to the other sacraments. Through Baptism we are freed from sin and reborn as sons of God; we become members of Christ, are incorporated into the Church and made sharers in her mission. (*CCC* 1213)

The sacrament of marriage is a human model of this relationship. As spouses totally give themselves to each other in marriage, they cease to be singles and instead begin a new life as one flesh, totally devoted to the other. "Since God created…man and woman, their mutual love becomes an image of the absolute and unfailing love with which God loves man" (*CCC* 1604).

My Journey from the World

From my earliest years, sports played a major role in my life. I have three older brothers who played soccer, and by the time I was six, I had begun to play too. Being the youngest certainly had its benefits. I was constantly trying to catch up and compete with my older brothers, who were bigger, stronger, and more skilled than I. This enabled me to develop my skills quickly and excel beyond my peers.

As time went on I began to get attention from people who recognized my skill level. Players and their parents were pleased that I was on their team. Soccer became more than a fun activity. I believed, at a young age, that I was valuable to others because I was good at this game.

I formulated a purpose and meaning for my life as I experienced the praise of others. I thought that I would truly be valuable if I became a professional soccer player. Soccer became the most important pursuit of my life; I gave myself completely to the game. Only when I got to high school would I realize that soccer had become my false god.

My family was one of those Catholic families who went to church and received the sacraments but struggled to make the faith a serious priority. My mother had a beautiful devotion to Jesus and to Mother Mary, but I did not embrace her love for them. How could I love someone I did not know? Jesus and Mary were merely characters from old stories. They lived in the past and had nothing to do with my life in the present.

My religious instruction was filled with great Bible stories, but the expectation was that I just believe they were true. I could not understand how all those stories of the past related to my current life. There was a huge disconnect. I believed that God created the world and that we would want to be with him when we died. But until then we were on our own. It was up to me to earn my way into heaven.

The sacrament of confirmation was a sort of graduation from church. I had jumped through all the Christian hoops, and now I could stop learning about God. The most exciting part of receiving the sacrament was that I was no longer obliged to attend classes. Now I had even more time to commit to soccer.

Honestly, Catholicism meant nothing to me. I kept going to Mass on Sundays but only because my mother required it.

The summer before my junior year of high school, I was invited to enter the Under-16 U.S. National Team tryouts. There were numerous levels of competition that culminated with a final trial in Jackson, Mississippi. After a grueling week of workouts, I was informed that I was one of the top eighteen players in the country.

My excitement at making the team was short-lived. The coach informed us that, due to budget cuts, there would be no team that year. I had been selected for a team that no longer existed!

In that moment my entire world was flipped upside down. I was angry, confused, and disillusioned. I was right where God wanted me!

I began to question everything. What was the purpose of my life? What could I possibly do if I did not play soccer? How could I be praised and loved if I was not a soccer star?

It took me a few months to work through what had happened and learn one of the greatest lessons of my life: If I place my value and worth in anyone or anything that can be taken away from me, I am placing my worth in the wrong place. Everything this world has to offer me can and will, in the end, be taken away from me.

Now a question arose: If my value does not come from what I have accomplished or what I possess, then where does it come from?

God was preparing to reveal himself to me. He began to surround me with disciples who would eventually lead me to him. Over the course of four months, I found myself at a Protestant religious program, where I encountered the Lord. I never knew I could experience the love of God in my heart as I did that night. The flood of emotions was like a tidal wave that picked me up and moved me to a place I had never been before. This experience of God's life in me was new, exciting, and captivating.

Like a farmer who tills the soil in preparation for planting seeds, God had been preparing me to receive the truth. Part of the process was to break apart the hardened areas of my past, tilling the soil to make room for new seeds of faith. I needed to see that my false god was not really a god at all. Soccer was only a game, which had no power to fulfill me. Not only did I need to cease pursuing soccer so that I would have time to find God, but I also had to be open to what God had to offer me.

I was so accustomed to earning love that I had no idea that I was inherently valuable and lovable by virtue of my creation. Within my heart was a quiet desperation, a longing for love and acceptance. This desperation had led me to give myself to people and activities (like soccer) with the hope that they would provide for me the love that I needed. Now God was offering me life and love in a way that I never had experienced before.

Regaining Our Hearts
God's plan is that we love people and use things. However, it seems that today we love things and use people, as if we were only objects and our hearts did not matter. The advancements in our world, while

helpful in many ways, have led many to a fake, plastic existence. The pressure to be acceptable according to the world's standards is so strong that people go to outrageous lengths to find the perfect look. We are consumed with this pretense and suppress the importance of our hearts and souls. We overlook the fact that we were created in God's image and therefore created to love.

We will never be happy until we are free to love. This freedom is a powerful gift from God. But sin and brokenness have created an atmosphere that suffocates love. The pain of this environment demands self-protection. We build walls in our hearts and create masks to hide who we truly are. We try to appear happy, whole, and fulfilled.

Closing off our hearts leaves us alone and empty, and we look to the world and its pleasures to fill the void. We believe that money, material things, drugs or alcohol, or other people will fill this God-shaped void in our hearts. Yet what is the truth? The truth is that they really cannot fulfill our needs.

Have you ever noticed that too much consumption of material items can make you sick of them? You might love chocolate, but eating an unusual amount each day will soon diminish your appreciation of it. Money works the same way. It seems to offer boundless possibilities for our pleasure that in the end leave us empty.

> Why spend your money for what is not bread;
>> your wages for what does not satisfy? (Isaiah 55:2)

What about sex? The world tells us that sex is what love is all about. Yet there are those who have had their fill and still pine for something more. Why? Because we were created for something far beyond this world and all it contains.

Our hearts were made for God! This is why people are willing to leave all behind once they have given their hearts to God. That is how St. Paul was able to walk away from his prior life.

Shortly after my conversion in high school, my father and brothers were shocked to discover that I had given up my dream of playing soccer professionally. They could not understand why I had to choose between God and soccer. While morally the two were not opposed to each other, they were clearly competing for the attention of my heart. At the same time, soccer no longer had the appeal it once had.

The decision to divert my attention from soccer toward God was very peaceful. I could see what my heart's true desire was. Drawing close to Jesus gave me the freedom to love.

The Struggle for Freedom

Every individual who chooses to become a disciple of Jesus Christ will struggle to let go of the world. Although an encounter with God is a powerful experience, it does not make the journey easy. We have grown quite accustomed to all this world has to offer. Each of us has our own unique disordered attachments that the Holy Spirit will reveal. They are disordered because they play too big a role in our lives, consuming too much of our time, energy, and focus. If we are not careful, we grow dependent upon whatever our attachments are. Our perceived need for them is so strong that we believe we can't live without them.

This predicament can be likened to a math exam. With sixty questions and only sixty minutes allotted for the test, we have an average of one minute per question. A disordered attachment leads one to spend thirty minutes on one question. This leaves very little time for the rest of the questions. We must learn to strike a balance in our lives, so we can allot time for all that is truly needed. Conversion in Christ causes a reorientation in our lives as new priorities are presented.

I love to sleep, and back in high school I often slept in as late as I could. Then, with barely enough time to grab a quick breakfast, I was out the door and running to school. After encountering Jesus, I found myself with new priorities: I wanted to spend time in prayer and Scripture study. I tried to do this every night, but it was just not happening. I was too exhausted by the time I got into my room each night. The result was that my relationship with Jesus was suffering.

The stage was set for the battle of self-denial. The Spirit called me to move my prayer time to the morning. That shift in schedule not only required me to get up earlier but also to deny myself activities at night. The inclusion of a new activity with God had a ripple effect throughout my day.

I started my new discipline strong, but after a couple of days I was sleeping in again. Thus began the cycle of praying for a few days, then falling back into laziness. It was in the midst of this struggle that I had to choose which was more important to me, my sleep or my relationship with Jesus. When deciding for Jesus, I discovered that my love for him was a powerful motivator to fight against my disordered life.

Although we were created in God's image and were designed to love with all our hearts and souls, we cannot gain the discipline of perfect self-control on our own. We need a relationship with the Holy Spirit. Galatians 5 tells us that a fruit of being with the Spirit is "self-control" (Galatians 5:23). We need God to help us let go of sin and disorders of the world so that we might draw close to him.

In the decision to choose God and to ask for his help, we gain the strength to fight for freedom. Once we have sufficiently tasted of this eternal life of love, we find the resolve to let go of worldly things we really don't need. Our desire for sharing in God's life grows the more we experience him. Our hearts resonate with words from a traditional Christmas song:

> Long lay the world in sin and error pining,
> till He appeared and the soul felt its worth.[4]

CHAPTER FIVE

Be Holy

• Deacon Ralph •

"Teacher, this woman was caught in the very act of committing adultery. Now in the law, Moses commanded us to stone such women. So what do you say?" They said this to test him, so that they could have some charge to bring against him. Jesus bent down and began to write on the ground with his finger. "Let the one among you who is without sin be the first to throw a stone at her." Again he bent down and wrote on the ground. And in response, they went away one by one, beginning with the elders. So he was left alone with the woman before him. Then Jesus straightened up and said to her, "Woman, where are they? Has no one condemned you?" She replied, "No one, sir." Then Jesus said, "Neither do I condemn you. Go, [and] from now on do not sin any more." (John 8:4–11)

✤The woman caught in the act of adultery was not prepared for what would unfold as she encountered Jesus. Those caught in adultery were to be stoned, so she could assume that she would die that day. The religious leaders were prepared to sacrifice her life and at the same time trap Jesus with this particular point of the law.

However, Jesus the Good Shepherd was not going to lose his little lamb. Not only would he spare her life, but he would impact that life to bring about radical change. His profound love would help her understand that she was called to live a better life than what she had settled for.

Encountering Jesus is not just a meeting or an introduction or even a connection of minds. It is a meeting of hearts that brings about a life-changing conversion. Like the woman in the Gospel of John, we cannot help but be changed when our hearts embrace the heart of Jesus. In that embrace comes a powerful love that enables us to not only see the truth of our lives but to accept it.

Now, accepting the truth intellectually can be challenging enough. But choosing to live that truth engages us in a lifelong battle requiring God's grace and our firm resolve. The fruits of his powerful love will be most fully experienced in our transformation from sinner to saint.

Seeing the Landscape

A study of history shows that our world has, at different periods of time, adopted various philosophies or schools of thought to distinguish truth. One of the oldest philosophies is called hedonism. Hedonism has two major objectives: the avoidance of pain and the pursuit of pleasure. This school of thought has been around for ages; it predates Christianity.

Hedonism has influenced many over the centuries. Some Christians are even led to believe that they can live by that philosophy. This idea could not be any further from the truth. Christ calls us to deny ourselves, pick up our cross and follow him (see Matthew 16:24). Life according to hedonism would have us avoid our crosses, to flee at the very first signs of their presence.

It appears as though hedonism has penetrated every walk of life and has become the authority for many of our decisions. While enjoying things that are pleasurable and avoiding pain are not necessarily wrong, they are problems once sin enters the scene.

The problems surface for those who encounter Christ. Once we receive the Holy Spirit, he sheds his light on areas of our lives that are not well ordered and are in need of correction. This is where the battle begins. It is a fight to move from a life of sin to the life God desires for us.

Ever since Adam and Eve sinned, humanity has been separated from God. It is more normal for us to live without God than it is to live with him. This norm is a deception, a powerful habit from which we must break free. Yet we cannot see past the deception and learn how to conquer this habit without God's help. We need the Spirit's assistance to see the truth and live a new life with God.

All things are possible for God (see Luke 1:37), but this does not mean it will be easy for us to make this paradigm shift. We must learn to be constantly aware of his presence in our lives.

The World's Games

This forces a confrontation with other powerful realities that influence our everyday decisions. The world and its forces are at work in our environment, shaping our lives. There are systems that help define us as a culture, and within these systems are pursuits that dominate us.

For example, our culture teaches us to value education as the ultimate means of attaining financial security. Our children go to school, and we parents are expected to demand good grades. We encourage children to graduate from high school, go to a good college, be successful, get a good job, and make a lot of money. Our children are formed to pursue money, for money is seen as the only source of security in this world.

In my travels all over the country, I encounter men who have fallen into the trap of believing that the man is the provider for the family. In many cases men spend hours away from their families pursuing financial security. While this is not inherently wrong, it often requires their wives to take care of all domestic issues, including the spiritual raising of the children. Much of a father's time can be lost because he is so busy making money.

What do we do with the fact that God declares himself the provider? In the covenant that God made with man through Abraham, he said, I will be your God and provide for all your needs, and you will be my people and will obey my commands (see Genesis 17). Jesus told us that we cannot serve two masters: We cannot serve both God and money (Matthew 6:24).

Where is the balance? Are we asking the tough questions in regard to our needs or our wants? We husbands are called to work, but our primary focus is to lead our spouses and children to the heart of God. This includes trusting that, as we seek first God's kingdom and his righteousness, he will take care of our needs (Matthew 6:33).

Another potentially dangerous formation that comes from hedonistic thought concerns how we deal with pain. We build walls to protect our hearts, and we demonstrate false pretenses in public to make it appear that we have our life together. These walls and masks characterize the angst of self-protection. Whereas we were created to live the truth, these methods of protection lead us to live lies.

Many of us experienced the cruelty of peers at a young age. Remember the rhyme about words not being harmful: "Sticks and stones may break my bones, but words will never hurt me"? The utterance of this phrase was considered protection from unkind remarks. As we grew older and wiser, our phrases became more sophisticated, with the likes of "Out of sight, out of mind" and "Time heals all wounds." Are these statements really true? Do we believe them so much as to live them?

The truth is that painful words do hurt, and wounds remain even if we try to suppress their memory. As much as we try to pretend that life is pain-free, that we can protect ourselves from the sin and cruelty of others, the facts remain. We do not live in truth if we follow the world's instructions for dealing with pain.

The Consequences of Sin

When God created humanity, our passions (or the flesh) were ordered and controlled by the spirit. With original sin we lost the sanctifying grace that enabled us to control the passions of the flesh. Basically, humanity lost the life of God within that enabled us to rightly manage our desires. We were left to rely on self-control of our own making rather than the self-control that the Spirit of God produces (see Galatians 5:22–23).

The absence of sanctifying grace created an environment that nurtures disordered desires for things and activities. Many of these desires are opposed to the life and will of God. St. Paul goes so far as to say, "Those who are in the flesh cannot please God" (Romans 8:8).

We see a natural example of this when observing the eating habits of children. Despite their physical needs for nutrition, they prefer to eat chocolate, ice cream, French fries, and chips. Many parents embark on dreadful battles with little ones who refuse to eat vegetables and other healthy foods once their taste buds have been enlightened to prefer sweets and junk food. Children easily develop disordered attachments to foods that should be limited.

It would be reasonable to imagine that as children grow up they would grow out of bad eating habits. But do they? We adults have a clear understanding of what our diets should consist of. We know the balance between the healthy and the not so healthy, right? But do disorders continue?

Perhaps rather than going away, disorders and passions change as we embark on adulthood. In fact, the objects of our passions may become more dangerous, even destructive to our physical, emotional, and spiritual well-being.

Each person has weaknesses within his or her own flesh. One person is attracted to a particular vice, while another is pulled to something quite different. Yet in each of us there lie vulnerabilities that are results of original sin.

Many of our passions are not sinful in themselves, but we lack control over them, and they consume our time. When we give in to them, with little or no restraint, they may cause problems for us. Perhaps we want to give more time to our newfound friend, Jesus, but we have no time to give. The number one reason why disciples do not pray is because they are too busy!

We All Have Enemies

Satan and demons really do exist. I am finding an alarmingly large number of people who have no idea of their existence. Satan and his demons were defeated when Jesus died on the cross, but they can still cause tremendous pain and suffering in humans when given the opportunity.

The greatest causes of infestation of demonic influence are ignorance of spiritual truth and absence of faith. For example, when a novel that depicts a secret romantic relationship between Jesus and Mary Magdalene exploded into pop culture, many people accepted the possibility that this could be true. Ignorance of spiritual truth let a naive public be easily led astray by false ideas. It did not take long for authorities, both within the Church and the secular world, to publicly reject the story's plausibility.

I remember giving a workshop to three hundred middle school students on this subject. While I used well-known secular sources to disprove the notions that this novel presents, these students were quick to respond with the simple phrase "It could happen." Their total disregard for logic was astounding. They argued that because they could think or imagine it, it could be true.

If this line of reasoning were valid, I could simply declare you to be an alien because I can imagine you as one. The power of suggestion is often a tool of the enemy, encouraging multitudes to disregard the truth and the role of logic in recognizing truth. He often does this behind the scenes, so the mistaken notion appears to be of human origin.

Before one encounters the Lord, the enemy remains hidden (in the dark), and he prefers to stay that way. The demons hope we will never discover their often subtle and silent attempts to keep us away from God and his Church. However, when one encounters holiness, the light of truth exposes the enemy.

Thus thwarted, Satan and his demons often change their tactic to that of fear. They try to make us believe that they can get us. Yet the truth of our faith is that we have authority over them when we invoke the name of Jesus. "Jesus is the devil's conqueror; he 'binds the strong man' to take back his plunder" (*CCC* 539; see Mark 3:27).

Return to Holiness

For the woman caught in adultery, an encounter with the Lord enabled her to recognize the true desires of her heart along with the web of deception woven by the enemy. This led her to a powerful conversion. Equipped with the truth, she was empowered to exercise authority to reject evil and seek holiness. She began to live as she was created to live.

Returning to a life of truth allows us opportunities to practice self-control with the help of the Holy Spirit. He enables us to live in holiness and align our behaviors with the will of God. We gain control of our passions and bring them into proper order. While we may still be tempted to over-engage in a particular passion, we have the spiritual strength needed to say no to that false pleasure. In our relationship with God, we gain the light to see the truth, the strength to deny ourselves, and the love that motivates us to seek perfection.

Yet there is still much more work to be done. Choosing to follow Jesus is a decision to enter into an interior battle. We often must fight against ourselves. With the help of the Holy Spirit, we can not only engage in the battle but also find victory and control. It will not be easy, but we are worth the effort. Jesus proved our inestimable worth with his sacrifice on the cross.

What is absolutely essential is that we continue to grow closer to the Lord and learn how to follow him. If we try to curb our passions without this interior development, we will fail, because we lack the life and strength of God that enables us to become holy. This is why every disciple must strive to develop his or her interior life with Jesus.

CHAPTER SIX

Entering the Silence
• *Fr. Dave* •

He was praying in a certain place, and when he had finished, one of his disciples said to him, "Lord, teach us to pray." (Luke11:1)

Scripture does not tell us the number of times the disciples encountered Jesus praying. But a brief search of Scripture yields several occasions on which Jesus prayed (see, for example, Matthew 14:23; Mark 14:32; Luke 6:12; John 17). What must it have been like to watch Jesus pray?

How significant it is that Jesus, the Son of God, the anointed one, the Messiah, felt the need to pray. Maybe, just maybe, we need to pray more!

The disciples wanted to do what Jesus did; they wanted to pray as he prayed. I imagine that when they approached Jesus, it was not out of mere curiosity: "We were wondering how to pray." Rather, "We want to do what you do. We have been paying attention (sometimes) and have come to understand that something happens to you when you pray. You know how to spend time with your Father. Jesus, teach us to do what you do."

A Gift Given

I'm not sure why, but prayer has always been important to me. Well, I guess I do know why: It's a gift that God gave me.

I remember as a kid, long after my mom and dad stopped helping me with my prayers, I would kneel down next to my bed and chat with God. As a child and a teen, my prayer was rather simple: "Thank you for another day. Bless my family. Help me pass my exam, which I kind of forgot to study for. Help me do better tomorrow. Let Notre Dame win on Saturday."

You know, the usual prayers of youth. I often used memorized prayers, but never a day went by that I did not talk with God. While it was good that I did that, at times I would think there had to be more.

Prayer has not come without its difficulties. I experienced this early in my priesthood. I wasn't praying as I should. In one sense I was just going through the motions. I think I got caught up in all the exciting things of priesthood and in its busyness. Believe it or not, Sunday morning is not the only time a priest works.

That's not to say that I wasn't praying at all. I celebrated Mass every day, prayed the Divine Office, and prayed with my fellow friars in the morning and evening. I would also pray as I prepared homilies. But I was not spending enough time with Jesus in personal prayer.

Much of my prayer was merely functional: I was attempting to accomplish something. I was getting my prayer in. I was always doing something when I prayed, rather than simply spending time with God. I wasn't being quiet, being present, and listening to the Lord.

This all changed in a few wonderful moments. While on an evangelization trip in Kenya, I concelebrated Mass with a local bishop. During his homily he stated, "God will give you gifts, and if you don't use them, he will look to some else who will. He is a good God and won't make you use his gifts, but he will find someone who will."

Tears welled up in my eyes. I knew the bishop was talking to me, and I knew prayer was the gift of which he spoke. God had gifted me, and I was not doing my part. I was not praying the way Jesus prayed.

It may be a stretch to say that Jesus took me all the way to Africa in order to hear that homily from the bishop, but I know that it changed me. I committed myself to changing the way I prayed.

Just Pray

In prayer we create the possibility of encountering God in a unique and special way. This is one of the primary reasons we pray. I pray to make myself available for an encounter with God.

This does not mean that every time I pray, I have a memorable encounter with God. But every time I pray, I make myself, to one degree or another, available for this encounter. The key is a desire to be present to God. It is impossible for me to encounter God if I don't make myself available to him.

Prayer is probably the most talked about and least done exercise in the spiritual life. This is unfortunate, because it is essential to the life of a disciple. If we want to encounter Jesus more in our daily lives, we must make ourselves available to him in prayer. It is inconsistent to say that we love God and want to follow him but don't pray. We are not able to grow in the spiritual life if we are not praying.

When beginning a life of prayer, one is faced with lots of questions. Why pray? How do I pray? When or how long should I pray? These are all good questions, but the most important is, when will I start? I suggest today. Just start.

Many people have shared with me that they put off prayer because they were not sure how to do it. I've repeatedly heard, "I don't want to do it wrong."

I'm not sure you *can* pray wrong. Just begin. Make a decision to begin a prayer life. Honestly, it may be one of the most important decisions you will ever make. We have to be very intentional about our prayer life; it is not going to magically happen.

If you desire to pray, it will be extremely helpful to make a plan. When you develop a plan for your prayer, it's important to be realistic and reasonable. If someone is terribly out of shape and wants to begin exercise, he doesn't try to run a marathon on the first day. In the same way, it may not be wise to shoot for an hour of personal prayer when you are just beginning. Maybe ten or fifteen minutes would be better. Start small, experience some success, and move on from there.

Ritually Speaking

Rituals are important to every culture and people. Next time you watch a football game, pay attention to the ritual of it all. Two sets of chosen players, dressed in a type of armor of their particular colors, march to the middle of the arena to face one another. Also present are a group of men dressed in zebra-like outfits, whose job it is to maintain order and to serve as objects of scorn to all those viewing the spectacle. A coin is flipped, a call is made, and sides are chosen to be defended. The uniforms, the symbols, the movement: It's all ritual.

Humans need ritual. Imagine a baseball game starting before someone yells, "Play ball." Unimaginable, right? In the same way, ritual helps us to pray.

We Catholics see this in our liturgy. There are things that make it our ritual. Priest, people, uniforms, candles, music, stories, movement, a beginning, and an end—these are all part of our tradition. Ritual provides a comfort in its familiarity.

One simple ritual I find helpful is how I begin and end my prayer. This is probably totally obvious, but prayer needs to have a beginning and an end. I am unbelievably fortunate to have a chapel wherever I live. When I go to the chapel it is to pray, and when I leave the chapel my prayer is finished.

However, I don't only pray in the chapel. I really love the text in the Bible where Jesus says to go to your room and pray (see Matthew 6:6). I often pray in my room, and I have a small oil candle there. When I begin my prayer, I light the candle. I don't light it because I love fire (but I kind of do) or because it looks cool (but it kind of does). My lighting it is my marking of time.

This time is different; it is time for prayer. This is my time with God. I am making myself available to him. When I blow the candle out, I am finished with my prayer. While this is a very simple ritual, over the years it has been beautifully successful in helping me pray.

How about you? Is there a quiet place in your home where you will meet the Lord? Maybe there's a special chair that will be your prayer chair.

Carving out a time of day is a good idea: Maybe every morning from 7:15 A.M. to 7:45 A.M. is your prayer time. Give it some reflection, be creative, make your prayer time personal, and then begin praying.

Make your own rituals. Consider stopping by your church on the way to get groceries. Or perhaps once a week, visit a chapel on the way home from work. Look for times and places to encounter God in prayer.

A Time for Devotions

I often experience the beauty of rituals when I practice various devotions. Devotionals can be a tremendous blessing to our growth in prayer because they offer a familiarity that helps us to relax and be at peace, much like being with an old friend.

Devotion to our Blessed Mother and the rosary is probably the most common devotion and can be a tremendous asset to growth in the spiritual life. Being able to meditate on the mysteries of the rosary provides great opportunities to draw us deeper into the central mysteries of our faith. It also provides occasions for us to cultivate discipline, which is a wonderful virtue in the spiritual life.

Novenas, chaplets, and other personal devotions may also be beneficial. If there is a particular devotion that speaks to your heart and draws you closer to the Lord, then take advantage of this. With that being said, my experience has taught me that oftentimes Catholics become extremely devoted to their particular devotion. In their zeal they are sometimes convinced that everyone else should share the same passion. At times this may be misguided. If you want to try a particular devotion, that's great. It if produces fruit in your spiritual life, thank the Lord for the blessing. However, one ought not feel compelled to participate in a personal or private devotion.

My experience is that there are seasons to devotions. There have been times in my life where a particular devotion has been a tremendous source of blessing to me for which I am truly grateful. The Chaplet of Divine Mercy is one example. During certain times in my life I have prayed the chaplet regularly and been very blessed by this. However, I don't feel I have to pray the chaplet every day. The season may come and go, and I am fine with that.

I have met many people who struggle with devotions. Some seem to be trapped in doing a particular devotion. For some people it borders on superstition, which is not healthy. Others fall into a type of multiplication of devotions. If one is good, then two or three must be better. There needs to be a balance here. When we begin a devotion, it doesn't mean that we are bound to it for the rest of our lives. Nor should we necessarily simply float from devotion to devotion on a whim. Rather, we discern the fruit of a particular devotion and proceed accordingly. We may continue if the devotion seems to produce grace; if not, perhaps it's time to try something else.

By the Way…

Distractions are a part of prayer. It is both amazing and scary what can enter into my mind when I am praying. A spiritual director once told me, "If you want to make sure you don't have distractions in your prayer, then stop praying, and you won't have any more distractions."

I actually like it when someone tells me that he or she is struggling with distractions in prayer. This says that the person is praying or at least trying to pray. That's much of the battle. The point is, distractions are a part of prayer, and we should not be surprised when they come. However, we can minimize them.

Ways of getting rid of distractions are probably as varied as the actual distractions. Over the years I have explored several different methods of dealing with these mental minefields. Here are several approaches, along with my critiques of them!

Force Field Model

This model attempts to build a force field around the person praying. The goal is to keep the distractions at bay. When distractions come, they won't be able to penetrate the holy force field and therefore won't bother the person praying.

This model may work for some, but for me it doesn't. I find myself spending most of my time keeping the force field engaged. I keep pushing the distractions away, trying to make sure nothing gets close to me. I worry about not being distracted and don't pray well.

Dial-in Model

In this model the individual is like a dialed-in laser beam. By sheer strength of intellect, the person is able to persevere in prayer no matter what. He or she is so focused on prayer that distractions simply have no power.

This model never works for me, maybe because I have the attention span of a gnat with attention deficit disorder. While I do attempt to focus in prayer (and this is important), that doesn't keep away all distractions.

Sift Model

This method works for me. I focus on prayer but am fully aware that distractions are going to come. When they come I let them go, like flour through a sieve. The distraction enters and is gone.

How one lets the distraction go is up to the person praying. I find it helpful to have some type of action or ritual, even if only imaginary, that surrenders the distraction. This could be laying the distraction before the feet of the Lord, placing it on an altar, putting it into a flowing river of grace, or anything I can imagine that lets the distraction depart.

After time and practice, this becomes a seamless process: The distraction comes, and I let it go; another comes, and I let it go. Sometimes something miraculous happens: I get to a place where no distractions come. My mind and my heart are quiet. It is there that I encounter God. He is there in the silence. It is a beautiful thing.

Finally, at times my distractions actually reveal something that God wants to say. If I am continually distracted about the same thing—say, something about the future—it may be that God wants to speak to me about trust. So while I don't focus a lot on my distractions, I am open to God speaking to me through them.

A Vital Necessity

Ultimately what is important about your prayer is that you not give up or get discouraged. Some days you will find prayer a delight, while other days you will struggle to sit down with God, stay awake, and keep your mind on him. You may wonder why you bother. Don't stop praying. All the struggles are normal parts of prayer. Be at peace, and ease in prayer will come.

> *Prayer is a vital necessity.* Proof from the contrary is no less convincing: if we do not allow the Spirit to lead us, we fall back into the slavery of sin [see Galatians 5:16–25]. How can the Holy Spirit be our life if our heart is far from him?
>
> Nothing is equal to prayer; for what is impossible it makes possible, what is difficult, easy [St. John Chrysostom]. (*CCC* 2744)

CHAPTER SEVEN

Prayer Encounters

• Fr. Dave •

I, too, hearing of your faith in the Lord Jesus and of your love for all the holy ones, do not cease giving thanks for you, remembering you in my prayers, that the God of our Lord Jesus Christ, the Father of glory, may give you a spirit of wisdom and revelation resulting in knowledge of him. May the eyes of [your] hearts be enlightened, that you may know what is the hope that belongs to his call, what are the riches of glory in his inheritance among the holy ones, and what is the surpassing greatness of his power for us who believe, in accord with the exercise of his great might. (Ephesians 1:15–19)

Not everyone is going to pray the same way. I don't expect my brother to have the same prayer life that I do. That simply is not realistic. We are individuals, and God relates to us as individuals.

One of the burdens that some experience as they desire to grow in the spiritual life is that most models of faith are priests and religious, whose lives seem more compatible with prayer. But a life of prayer is not only for priests and religious. Everyone should seek to have an active prayer life.

I wouldn't expect busy moms to pray in the same way Mother Teresa prayed. But this is not to say that they can't pray at all. Rather they need to prayerfully consider their circumstances and discern what type of prayer life God is inviting them to have.

Also there are seasons to a prayer life. When I visit my parents, I see them begin each morning with an extended prayer time over a cup of coffee or two. It is delightfully silent and peaceful. It has not always been that way. Their prayer years ago, with six teenagers storming around the house, was quite different from what they experience now.

Be Yourself

Only you, in dialogue with God, can determine how you should pray. Spending time with God each day is important, but what that looks like will be up to you and him.

It's always a good idea to start the day off with some kind of morning offering. This keeps us focused and reminds us of God's presence during the day. Devotions are tremendous gifts to the Church and may be a blessing to your prayer. They can help you stay connected to God. The rituals, patterns, and formats can all be very good, freeing you from the need to figure out what to do or say.

This is not to say that when we pray the rosary, Divine Mercy Chaplet, or a novena we don't think about what we are doing. Rather, we don't have to think about *how* to do what we are doing. A repetitive devotion helps clear our minds and open us to encountering God. At times I experience this as being swept away in a very moving and powerful experience of the presence of the Lord. Also, during particularly dry times in our spiritual life, devotions keep us grounded and help us to not quit.

Spiritual reading and study are also very beneficial. It is a sad but true fact that for many Catholics, spiritual formation stopped twenty minutes after they were confirmed. Whether this was in high school or grade school, the unfortunate reality is that there has been very little intellectual faith development in their adult life.

Imagine if you were stuck in a high school mind-set in other areas of your life. Scary, right? As we grow in our spiritual life, it's important that our hearts and minds develop. Take the time to read books, articles, papal documents, and the *Catechism of the Catholic Church.* You'll notice your mind growing, developing, and being filled with the Lord's grace.

Another practice I find helpful is keeping a prayer journal. This is different from a diary: I don't write down what has happened in my day. Rather it is a journal in which I recount what I think God is saying to me and what I want to say to him. I also keep a list of people and things that I have said I would remember in prayer.

I might write in the journal a couple times a week or maybe only once a month. It is not something I feel obligated to do all the time, but over the years it has been a very fruitful exercise.

Speak, Lord

No one can ever say that God doesn't speak to him or her. The Scriptures are the living Word of God, and every time we sit down to pray with the Scriptures, we encounter God. It's important that we become familiar with the Scriptures. Recall what St. Jerome famously said, "Ignorance of the Scriptures is ignorance of Christ."[5] We need to be familiar with the stories of Scripture and allow them to give direction to our lives.

Ask God to help you approach the Scriptures with great faith. Far too often people come to Scripture not expecting God to reveal anything to them. If that is your attitude, then it is exactly what you will get. However, it does not have to be that way.

God is present in his Word and wants to be present to us through it. We ought to pray before we read the Scriptures and ask God to show himself to us.

When people come to me for spiritual direction the first time, I always give them an exercise to complete before the next time we meet. I ask them to read 1 John. It's only five brief chapters, and it is really a beautiful book. In many ways it is the Gospel in a nutshell.

I encourage you to do this: Make the decision to read 1 John. Before you sit down to read it, ask the light of the Holy Spirit to bless and fill you. Pray that the Spirit of Jesus will illuminate your mind and that the Word of God will penetrate your heart. Then read the entire book. It shouldn't take much more than fifteen minutes.

For the following week spend time going over 1 John slowly and in depth. Take a few minutes each day to read a chapter or a part of a chapter, and then reflect on what it says. Ask yourself, "What does this say to me? What does this tell me about God? What does this tell me about myself?"

Another thing I find helpful every now and then is to read the Scriptures out loud. Even if only in a whisper, there is something moving about reading the Scriptures aloud. To hear the Word of God is a blessing, and to have it come from my own lips is a double grace.

All of the Scriptures are inspired, but not all are equally inspiring. The Gospels should inspire us; read them and familiarize yourself with the many stories of Jesus. Place yourself in the various scenes. Close your eyes and see yourself in the crowd.

Let your imagination be directed by God. What does Jesus look like? How about the people with whom he is relating? Where are you in the story? What surprised you, or what didn't you expect?

Get to know the Jesus of the Scriptures. Have a favorite story, a favorite parable, and a favorite verse. It's good to memorize a few of your favorite passages. Having the Word of God on your lips is a powerful tool in times of hardship and temptation.

That being said, I am always inspired by people who are able to quote all kinds of Scripture, chapter and verse, but that isn't me. I guess my mind doesn't work that way. I can quote the ones that have had the greatest impact in my life, and I am good with that.

A Whole Life of Prayer

While it is important to pray daily, it's also good to consider your prayer life as a whole, not only in twenty-four-hour periods. We are striving for a life of prayer, not only a prayer day. When thinking about a prayer life, look at your day but also at your week, month, and year.

When looking at your week, see if there may be a time when you could take a holy hour at the church or chapel of your choice. More and more churches are offering Eucharistic Adoration, which is a source of countless blessings. Consider committing yourself to a weekly holy hour.

I know of an extremely busy attorney, the father of four, who takes a holy hour every Saturday at 4:00 A.M. He states that while it is at times difficult to make the holy hour, it is important for him to give this commitment to the Lord, and the early morning time works best for his hectic schedule. No doubt the Lord blesses his effort.

If a weekly holy hour at your church is not possible, consider simply stopping by the church for a few minutes on the way to or from work, an errand, or picking up groceries. It may seem odd, but I believe that there is a special grace in getting out of your car, walking into the church, and spending a few minutes with the Lord. It causes you to be intentional about spending time with the Lord, which I think is important in the spiritual life.

Prayerfully consider attending Mass one time a week other than Sunday. Being able to receive Jesus in the Eucharist during the week is a great help in the spiritual life.

When looking at your month, think about blocking out a few hours for a personal retreat. This does not have to be a complicated thing: Just get away from your routine for a couple hours of extended time with God. Be creative. Maybe make a pilgrimage to your cathedral for Mass, confession, and prayer.

I love the idea of making mini-pilgrimages a part of my life. When possible I visit the cathedral in whatever diocese I am visiting. Perhaps a retreat center, a monastery, or a convent is available. Many religious communities welcome guests who want to pray in their chapels, so don't be shy about inquiring about such possibilities.

For some people, getting away from the city and going to a lake is a blessed retreat. Whatever works for you is great. Just try once a month to get away for a bit of an extended time with the Lord.

Finally, try to make a weekend retreat part of your yearly schedule. My father was a busy physician, and he took at least one weekend retreat, usually more, every year. He knew it was important for him to have that time away from work and even family in order to focus and be present to God.

Many parishes and dioceses offer retreats, so take advantage of those opportunities. You will be richly blessed.

Deeper Still

The mind or intellect is important when we pray, but there is more than that. Every human person has a soul; that's actually part of what makes us human. We are not only flesh and bone, but we are also spirit. God breathes in each of us a soul, and that soul is eternal.

We don't generally reflect a lot about our souls. But think about this for a minute. You have within you a soul that will always be. For the rest of eternity, your soul will exist.

So often our prayer is only an intellectual exercise. We think about God, think about holy things, and think about for whom we should pray. Now, there is nothing wrong with this; it is actually a very important part of prayer. But sometimes we can move from praying only from our mind to praying with our soul or our heart.

I say sometimes, because to pray like this takes practice, time, and work. To pray from our soul we need to be silent. This is more than not talking; it involves our tuning out the world, noise, distractions, even ourselves, and being still before God. I am reminded of Psalm 46:10: "Be still and know that I am God!" In the quiet, the stillness, we can discover God.

It's pretty amazing actually. When we are able to pray from our eternal soul, we experience a union with the eternal God. Most often we don't hear God say anything; we don't get some directive for our lives; we just experience God's presence. And this is prayer: a simple encounter with the God of the universe, who more than anything wants to be close to us.

The first time I went snorkeling in the ocean, off the coast of Guam, I placed a mask on my face and looked into the water and discovered a whole new world. There were colors such as I had never seen. The plants, fish, and other creatures were spectacular. There was an entire world that lived under the waves, which I had never seen before.

And so it is with an interior life. In prayer we are invited to discover a new world that lies beneath the surface of our lives. It takes some effort to be able to discover it, but once we do, we always want to return. May we return there time and time again to discover the living God.

CHAPTER EIGHT

Embracing the Cross

• *Fr. Dave* •

Then he said to all, "If anyone wishes to come after me, he must deny himself and take up his cross daily and follow me. For whoever wishes to save his life will lose it, but whoever loses his life for my sake will save it. What profit is there for one to gain the whole world yet lose or forfeit himself? Whoever is ashamed of me and of my words, the Son of Man will be ashamed of when he comes in his glory and in the glory of the Father and of the holy angels. Truly I say to you, there are some standing here who will not taste death until they see the kingdom of God." (Luke 9:23–27)

Following Jesus won't be easy. I suppose no one ever said it would be, but lots of people dance around the issue, trying not to get burned. Being a disciple of Jesus is the most amazing, rewarding, meaningful, satisfying, life-giving journey anyone can imagine. But it's hard. Really hard.

The author of Sirach wrote, "My child, when you come to serve the Lord, prepare yourself for trials" (Sirach 2:1). St. Peter tells us, "Beloved, do not be surprised that a trial by fire is occurring among you, as if something strange were happening to you" (1 Peter 4:12).

This is not to say that those who choose not to follow the Lord don't have trials, but a Christian's trials present a unique opportunity to encounter the suffering Christ. It may be that this encounter with Christ is the most profound and yet under-experienced meeting. Before one gets to that place, a few choices need to be made.

Denied

In Luke's Gospel (as well as in Matthew's and Mark's), Jesus says, "*If* you want to follow me deny yourself, pick up your cross daily and follow me." The first thing we have to wrestle with is the word *if*. It's up to you. Do you want to follow him?

I suppose people can make us do certain things, but no one can really make us follow Jesus. Jesus doesn't make us follow him; how can anyone else? Jesus invites but never forces. So each of us needs to deal with *if*. If we choose to follow Jesus, then we need to pay close attention to the condition he presents.

"If you want to follow me…"

"Yes, Jesus, I want to follow you; what now?"

"If you want to follow me, the first thing you need to do is deny yourself."

Consider this: The first condition offered in this text for following the Lord is not to stop sinning or to love more but rather to deny oneself. Is it possible that there is a connection between our ability to deny ourselves and living the life of a disciple? Here we read that not only is it possible, but this connection is essential.

There is a conflict between the inordinate cravings of the flesh and the Gospel. Why else would Jesus say, "Deny yourself"?

I experience this conflict from time to time. I wrestle with what I want to do and what God or perhaps someone else wants of me. I have known this tension since I was a child.

"David, you need to clean your room."

"Mommy, I don't want to clean my room."

"David, I don't recall asking what you wanted."

"Got it."

I am sure everyone has experienced a tension such as this: the internal struggle to do what you know needs to be done versus the flesh, which wants to do your own thing. This is particularly problematic in our walk with the Lord. Key to the spiritual life is our ability to die to self in order to allow God's will to be done in us. We must learn to turn from self to God.

No, Thank You

A graced source for practicing denial in my life has been fasting. It is something that has been a part of my life since I was young. My mom and I would fast on bread and water from Holy Thursday until the Easter vigil. (I also remember very fondly going out to eat after the vigil Mass. That is one of many family customs and celebrations that are dear to me.)

It's probably fair to say that my motivations for fasting were mixed. As a teen, I probably didn't recognize the deep spiritual significance of denying myself. But I did understand that what I was doing in some way connected me to Jesus. Plus I liked the fact that what I was doing was hard. For a teenager that was cool. Finally, I appreciated fasting with my mom. There was a special bond between us during that time.

Later I grew in my appreciation of fasting for others. I fast from sweets, soda, or snacks, perhaps for someone's conversion, healing, or special intention. In fasting I experience a connection to both God and the individuals for whom I am fasting. It is a very wonderful practice.

Over the years I have experienced similar graces in fasting with other people for particular intentions. There is a beautiful connection between disciples who choose to fast with each other for a common purpose.

When I turned thirty-three, I wanted to fast from something for the entire year. The Lord gave his life for me at thirty-three, and I wanted to offer a small sacrifice during this significant year. I was fully aware that nothing I offered could suffice, but I wanted to give something. After some prayer I decided that I would fast from alcohol. It wasn't that I drank a lot or often; it just seemed to be what God wanted.

As it turned out, this was the year I visited Italy for the first time. I suspect you know where this is going.

I recall my first day in Rome. The motherhouse of my Franciscan community sits on the Roman Forum. I walked onto our balcony and was treated to a spectacular view of the magnificent, historical buildings. I was kind of in a daze. I couldn't believe that I was actually in Rome, peering at the Roman Forum! The sun setting over the scene painted everything a magical red. Could this be any more incredible?

Apparently it could. The friars appeared with the most beautiful Italian cheese and salami along with an array of crackers and breads. Then came the final touch, the wine. The goblets glistened in the rays of the setting sun. The deep, rich red of the wine perfectly paired with the colors of the Forum. Never in my life had I so longed for wine, nor had there ever been a time more appropriate for it.

The friars began to pour me a glass (apparently in Italy you don't ask if someone wants wine, because the answer is always yes). Through a translator I explained that I did not care for any wine. The friar pouring the wine looked bewildered. I went on to explain that I was fasting. He glared at me with a look of pity and explained that one does not fast from wine. Oh, my.

My next stop, Germany, featured one of the best bratwursts I have ever had, washed down with the worst cola.

I have continued my birthday to birthday fast to this day. I have been blessed by the fast and also by the discernment process each year going into it. For a few weeks before my birthday, I pray about what the Lord is asking of me. My fast is not always from food but may be from other things I like. What is consistent year to year is simply denying myself of something.

This is a total fast, in that I don't break it on Sundays or special feast days. I know myself well. I could find a million reasons to break my fast if I allowed myself that option. "Groundhog Day! I love Groundhog Day. Call off the fast; let's celebrate!"

During the year I participate in other types of fasting. I generally don't eat meat on Fridays, and I fast during various liturgical seasons. I am extremely aware of how simple my fast is and am under no illusion that it is particularly difficult. My giving up a piece of cake, a soda, or sleep is not going to change the world. However, slowly, over time, I do pray that it changes *me*.

One way that I know it has changed me is that my fasting causes me to remember. In a very simple and poignant way, I am reminded that I can say no to desires of the flesh and say yes to God's will. I can die to myself in order to live for him.

When I am fasting I encounter Jesus, who continually said, "Not my will but yours be done" (Luke 22:42). If I want to follow Jesus, which I do, I need to be able to deny myself.

Even There

Why didn't God do something? Why did God let this happen? Is God here?

On a number of occasions, I have visited the death camp of Auschwitz in Poland. While I try to imagine the horrors that took place inside the barbed-wire fence surrounding the camp, I usually end up empty. There is nothing I have experienced that is able to bring me to a place of understanding.

On one visit I found myself alone outside of St. Maximilian Kolbe's cell. I tried to pray there, sitting on the damp, cold, concrete floor. I leaned my head against the steel bars of the cell, thinking about what had taken place there. A few votive candles flickered to break the darkness.

Rather than feeling sadness in this dark place, I experienced a sweet presence. "Lord, are you here? How is it you are in a place like this?"

I sensed Jesus saying to me, "How can I not be? My death on a cross means that I will always be in places like this."

There is no way to make sense out of what happened in Auschwitz. To try to make sense out of the senseless is an exercise in futility. If this is true for Auschwitz, how much more so for Jesus's death on a cross? Why the pain and suffering?

I suppose we will always have questions, but what we must keep in mind is that God is there. God reveals his love and power in the cross. To those without faith the cross is crazy, but to those with faith the cross is the very power of God (see 1 Corinthians 1:18).

The power of the cross is such that even in a cold, musty cell at Auschwitz, God can make himself known. That's where artist Mieczyslaus Koscielniak and other prisoners heard St. Maximilian speak of the faith. "We listened spellbound, temporarily forgetting our hunger and degradation."[6] Grace allowed them to encounter Jesus in a seemingly hopeless place.

The willingness to embrace the cross is perhaps the most telling indicator of the level of one's discipleship (if such things can be measured). Are we able to see Christ, to encounter him, in the midst of our pain and suffering? We must pick up our crosses daily—not just once and not just those big crosses that come only rarely. Most days our crosses will be disasters like being in the slow line at the grocery store, bouncing a check, or arguing with family.

But there may be crosses like cancer, divorce, miscarriage, and death, crosses that could take our very life-breath away. There may be crosses that bring the world to a halt and cast us into darkness. It is there that we ask questions like, God, where are you? Do you see? Do you notice? What now?

Here's the thing: Jesus is there. We may not be able to see or hear him, but he really is there. We are not alone.

Jesus desires to meet us in the midst of our pain and suffering. If we accept the invitation to die to our own will and accept the cross he presents, we can encounter him in a way that is truly life-changing. Our cross is transformed from something to be railed against to an encounter of grace and a place of hope. This is the beauty and majesty of the cross of Christ.

A Sweet Gift

When Jesus tells us that the life of a disciple involves a cross, he is making clear to us what we are going to encounter. The human condition involves suffering. Jesus chose to embrace the cross, and he invites us to do the same. When we are presented with difficulties, trials, and tribulations, we have a choice. How am I going to deal with this? Am I going to accept it and try to grow in love and virtue, or am I going to run away? With his grace we can embrace our cross and experience his presence. This is an encounter with Jesus that can be most unexpected and delightfully sweet.

While we certainly don't have to go looking for our crosses, we also need to stop running from them. Our cross, whatever it may be, is always an invitation to encounter Jesus. As we embrace all that Christ has for us, we encounter his healing power in our suffering, and our hearts begin to change. We no longer turn away from Jesus when we struggle but rather turn toward him. We discover the sweet presence of God in places we never knew or even imagined.

I know a woman who discovered such a place in the death of her father. A few days before his death, I had shared with Elizabeth that in the cross, in our suffering, we can encounter God. Elizabeth later wrote, "Fr. Dave, I didn't know that your words were going to prepare me and my family to encounter Christ." She went on to explain how her father's last three days of life were "a gift we will never be able to describe."

> My heart was ready to receive that gift.... My prayer for my dad was that he would encounter Christ in his last days, and there were many such encounters.... Dad's last minutes were full of power and glory that only the Lord can offer....
>
> The days after my dad's death we celebrated with great joy my dad's ultimate encounter with Christ.... What a gift my husband, daughter, and I experienced in encountering Christ in the midst of my father's death.

Yes, it is true. Through God's grace our hearts can move from fear of the cross to acceptance. When we allow this to happen, we can echo Elizabeth's beautiful words, "My heart was ready to receive the gift."

Lord Jesus, continue to break into our lives and make our hearts ready to receive the gift of your cross.

CHAPTER NINE

Encountering the Spirit
• *Deacon Ralph* •

When the time for Pentecost was fulfilled, they were all in one place together. And suddenly there came from the sky a noise like a strong driving wind, and it filled the entire house in which they were. Then there appeared to them tongues as of fire, which parted and came to rest on each one of them. And they were all filled with the Holy Spirit and began to speak in different tongues, as the Spirit enabled them to proclaim. (Acts 2:1–4)

⚜After the Ascension the apostles stood on the mountaintop remembering Jesus's words, "Behold, I am with you always, until the end of the age" (Matthew 28:20). They struggled to understand his meaning as they witnessed his ascension into heaven. How could he be with them if he just left?

I imagine one of them said, "I hate it when he does that." And after a couple of confused chuckles, they returned to Jerusalem to await the promised baptism of the Holy Spirit (see Acts 1:5). The apostles had learned to take Jesus at his word.

The Mystery of Oneness
The apostles went to the upper room, and there they prayed with expectant hearts. Although they anticipated the coming of the Holy

Spirit, they had no idea what a baptism in the Holy Spirit was like. You can imagine their astonishment when the Spirit came upon them.

The apostles were lit on fire with love for God. Their expectant hearts became wonderful dwelling places for the Spirit. This was not a warm, fuzzy experience of God. They received the awesome power of the Holy Spirit. As astounding as it was, there was something in that encounter that was strangely familiar.

One of my favorite questions to ask is, "When the Holy Spirit came upon the apostles at the Feast of Pentecost, who did the apostles recognize?" Most of the time I get blank stares, but once in a while someone will make the connection and say, "Jesus."

I believe this was one of the greatest aha moments the apostles experienced. The Lord they longed to be with more than anyone else had returned to their lives, only in a new way. His words before the Ascension came thundering back, "I will be with you always" (Matthew 28:20).

At Pentecost the apostles also gained instant understanding of the mystery of the Trinity. Jesus's words echoed back to them: "Whoever has seen me has seen the Father" (John 14:9); "The Father and I are one" (John 10:30). They understood that having the Holy Spirit actively living in their hearts was also to be with Jesus and with the Father!

One of the benefits of being a disciple of Jesus was serving him and being with him for three years. These men experienced face-to-face conversations with Jesus. During those years his eyes were upon each of them. They exchanged encouraging glances, shared in the grace of his laughter, and pondered the depths of his teachings. When Jesus spoke, the disciples experienced the human and divine life of their Savior.

Their encounters with the Lord on earth were not just physical encounters but also spiritual ones. Their time with him prepared them to recognize the divinity in this moment of Pentecost. Although they could no longer see the Lord physically, they recognized him spiritually. Like the disciples on the road to Emmaus (see Luke 24:13–35), the apostles must have experienced a burning in their hearts at the presence of the Spirit.

This profound reality confirmed their understanding and solidified their mission. Because of Pentecost, every heart created for God could now enter into union with him. Jesus's redemptive work had enabled the Holy Spirit to come. Now all those who received the Spirit would receive the Son and the Father as well. The plan to redeem the world and restore God's union with humanity was coming to fruition.

My Baptism in the Spirit

My initial encounter with the Lord was my first experience of the life of the Holy Spirit. Once I opened the door of my heart, the Spirit came flooding in and filled me with love and peace. I gained a new awareness of his presence as I engaged in my prayer life. My fellowship with other disciples in my church youth group helped me develop this new relationship with Jesus. I understood that in God's saving plan, this was the time for the Holy Spirit to work directly with me.

After high school I remained close to my faith community while attending a local junior college. I served as a volunteer youth leader at church. It was on a retreat with the leadership team that I was introduced to the baptism in the Holy Spirit.

The veteran leaders spoke of the Lord's desire to empower me for ministry and encouraged me to ask the Holy Spirit for gifts to serve. I had read John the Baptist's description of being baptized in the Spirit but never knew what that meant (see Matthew 3:11). I knew that I wanted to receive more from God.

The team offered to pray over me, and I approached this time of prayer with an open heart. It was a powerful moment in my life. I was overcome by the presence of the Lord. His power, like electricity, surged through me, and I began to pray in tongues. It was as if the Spirit had taken control of my mouth and tongue and began to form sounds. I could not understand what I was saying, but I had a strong sense of praise in my heart. I realized that I was praising God.

As if to prove to me that this experience was from the Lord, the Spirit spoke to my heart about an event that was about to happen in my life. He revealed to me that a particular situation was looming and that I needed to trust that he would see me through it, as long as I believed. The rest of the night was filled with great peace and affirmation in the Lord's desire for me.

I returned home to find that my girlfriend wanted to break up. This was what the Lord had warned me about. With a peace that could only come from God, I let her go. The Lord continued to work in my heart, and I slowly began to learn how to be fulfilled by the Spirit of the living God.

Life in the Spirit

We were created with both spirit and flesh, and in the beginning of time man's spirit was in total control of the flesh and passions. Due to original sin, we lost the life of God that was destined to dwell within us. Devoid of this grace, we grew accustomed to living solely in this earthly existence, with limited understanding of our spiritual capacity. Our nature is fallen and prone to sin.

Jesus restores us to a life of grace by his death on the cross. He gives us the Spirit of God, to empower us to live harmoniously in the physical and spiritual realms of life. The problem is that often-times either we don't let the Spirit help us or we are unaware of the Spirit's power to help. Yet we can't live a holy life, faithful to the Lord's commandments, without the help of the Holy Spirit.

I have experienced this time and time again in my own life. I genu-inely devote all of my efforts toward being holy, but I quickly fail. I figure if I just try harder, I can be holy. But oftentimes I lack the self-control necessary to live the way I know God wants me to live. This causes great angst and frustration, until I finally get the memo: "I am not capable of living the holy life without the life of God in me!" I need the help of the Holy Spirit and the fruits of the Spirit.

In the fifth chapter of Galatians, St. Paul lists the fruits of the Spirit: "The fruit of the Spirit is love, joy, peace, patience, kindness, generosity, faithfulness, gentleness, self-control Against such there is no law" (Galatians 5:22–23). I have discovered that the more time I spend with the Holy Spirit, the more fruit of his presence grows in my life. In particular, I have gained more self-control. Sinful passions and actions that I was not able to control on my own have yielded to the Spirit of God. With his power I am able to live a more Christ-centered, virtuous life.

In the saving plan of God, he sent his Son to atone for our sins. After Jesus's work was done, he returned to the Father so that the Spirit might be sent to us.

> When Christ is finally glorified [John 7:39], he can in turn send the Spirit from his place with the Father to those who believe in him: he communicates to them his glory [see John 17:22], that is, the Holy Spirit who glorifies him [John 16:14]. (*CCC* 690).

This is the time of the Holy Spirit. He is the one who will complete the good work Jesus began in us (see Philippians 1:6).

The Holy Spirit is the one who is charged with the task of restoring us to holiness; that is not our job. What are we supposed to do? The first task of every disciple is to constantly avail himself or herself of the Holy Spirit. The Catholic faith is all about regaining our relationship with God through the Holy Spirit.

Entering the School of the Holy Spirit

In high school I had the opportunity to take a woodworking class. I remember walking into the shop, which was filled with all kinds of machinery that I never knew existed. I could not wait to get my hands on those machines.

Ours was a wise instructor. He taught us how to manually do the craft of woodworking before we touched a single machine. As he introduced the various hand tools, he emphasized the procedures we needed to follow to keep us safe. With each tool came an awesome respect for the potential it had to complete simple tasks, like cutting off fingers. It did not take long for us to learn just how easy it was to cut, scrape, and tear the skin off our hands.

Our teacher constantly looked out for us, vigilantly catching those who were foolish with their tools. He would stop us, correct us, and encourage us to continue. He was ready with first aid supplies for those who had to learn the hard way. Only when he felt confident in our ability did he train us in how to use the power tools.

Entering into discipleship training is literally entering the school of the Holy Spirit. In this school the Spirit intentionally instructs us and leads us in our growth process. God desires to bring us into full knowledge and understanding of him, and he will use whatever and whomever he chooses. He is watchful and attentive, like my shop teacher. The Spirit starts with the basics of the spiritual life to nourish our growth in faith.

The Spirit develops in us the fruits of the Spirit: love, joy, peace, patience, kindness, generosity, faithfulness, gentleness, self-control. These fruits enable us to rightly discern the Spirit's guidance in situations.

For example, in life we encounter many fearful situations. In fact, we often make decisions based on fear. When we are in the Spirit's presence and in a state of grace, we can experience both fear and God's peace at the same time. When this happens we need not act on the fear. We can faithfully trust in the Spirit's peaceful presence and move with him through the fear.

The fruits are means by which we come to recognize the presence of the Spirit in our daily lives. However, we are not accustomed to working with the Spirit when we enter this training. We need assistance in learning how to harvest the fruits.

Mature disciples of Christ play key roles in helping new believers grow in their discernment of the Spirit's fruits. They help young disciples transition from a life of fear to a life in the Spirit. St. Paul instructed Timothy in this: "For God did not give us a spirit of cowardice but rather of power and love and self-control" (2 Timothy 1:7). The Spirit desires that each child of God learn how to walk in the confidence of the Father's presence.

Have you ever seen a child walk fearfully while they were with their loving parents? Of course not. Children trust that their parents will take care of them. So it is with those who live in the Spirit. They need not fear, knowing that God will take care of them. The fruits of the Spirit help us recognize that he is truly present with us.

Gaining confidence in God's presence and in our ability to rightly discern his fruits, we are open to growing deeper in faith. This openness allows the Spirit to empower us with his gifts. Like my shop teacher who taught me the basics, the Spirit teaches us how to use God's powerful gifts when we are ready for them. Some of these gifts are wisdom, understanding, counsel, knowledge, healing, prophecy, and discernment of spirits (see Isaiah 11:1–2; 1 Corinthians 12:8–10). These gifts are not for our own edification but for the building up of the kingdom of God. "Seek to have an abundance of them for building up the church" (1 Corinthians 14:12).

Equipped to Serve God's People

As we become docile to the Spirit's will, we are commissioned for specific tasks and given the powers (gifts) to accomplish them. We can count on this ever-present principle: If God sends us on a task, he is already providing us with the means to accomplish it. Although most of us will maintain that we feel ill-equipped for many of the tasks that God asks of us, God is fully prepared to accomplish those tasks through us. Even while we are serving him by ministering to others, he is always helping us to grow in faith. He does not call the equipped; he equips the called.

The day of my ordination to the permanent diaconate, I did not feel sufficiently equipped to serve the Church. But when the bishop ordained me, the Spirit confirmed this call in my heart with his fruits of love, joy, and peace.

My first year of ordained ministry was tenuous, since I was focused on my performance rather than on serving. I was fearful that God would not show up, leaving me to deliver a subpar performance. As I served in the various capacities of a deacon, the Lord was present, ministering to his people. Gradually I began to understand that I am simply a tool of the moment; God is always the minister. Once over that fearful hump, I was able to rest in the peace of the Spirit, knowing that God will always provide.

Trusting that God will empower us with his gifts to minister to others, we are prepared to be effective tools of the Spirit. We will accomplish things we never imagined when we allow God to flow through us. We may find an amazing rush of God's presence as we witness the Holy Spirit serving others through us.

Let us allow God to use us. The consequences are eternal.

CHAPTER TEN

Living for Others

• *Deacon Ralph* •

When he reached the place, Jesus looked up and said to him, "Zacchaeus, come down quickly, for today I must stay at your house." And he came down quickly and received him with joy. When they all saw this, they began to grumble, saying, "He has gone to stay at the house of a sinner." But Zacchaeus stood there and said to the Lord, "Behold, half of my possessions, Lord, I shall give to the poor, and if I have extorted anything from anyone I shall repay it four times over." And Jesus said to him, "Today salvation has come to this house because this man too is a descendant of Abraham. For the Son of Man has come to seek and to save what was lost." (Luke 19:5–10)

The Gospels contain numerous stories of dramatic encounters with Jesus that bring about instant transformations in people's lives. We see this in the story of Zacchaeus.

Zacchaeus was a tax collector, which meant that his own Jewish brethren did not accept him. Tax collectors were notorious for extorting money from the people in the name of Rome and keeping a share for themselves. The Jews were already upset about being a conquered people forced to pay taxes, so they looked down upon any fellow Jew who worked with the Romans and stole from his own people. They wanted to have nothing to do with Zacchaeus.

Jesus was traveling through the region, and the town was filled with excitement. The whole area was talking about the new holy man who spoke with authority and had the power to heal. Doubtless each person in town had his or her own hopes and dreams of what could happen in an encounter with him. Zacchaeus was no different. But since the righteous Jews excluded him, Zacchaeus could only hope to catch a glimpse of Jesus.

As Jesus approached the town, the crowds lined the streets in order to get close to him. Zacchaeus perhaps tried squeezing through the crowd but was rebuffed. Scripture tells us he was short in stature, so he did the only reasonable thing: He ran ahead and climbed a tree along Jesus's route.

It must have been odd to see a tax collector, a figurehead for Rome and one of the richest men in town, climbing a tree. But that is exactly what Zacchaeus did. And he was rewarded beyond his wildest dreams. Jesus not only acknowledged Zacchaeus by name but also told him that he desired to share a meal with him.

This invitation was significant. Table fellowship was a very intimate event within the Jewish culture. A holy man did not usually choose to be the guest of a sinner. Jesus reached out to Zacchaeus when no one else would.

In response to this encounter, Zacchaeus decided to give away what he had come to value most in life, his money. What would make a person give away half of all he owned? Love! In Jesus's simple gesture of kindness and acceptance, Zacchaeus felt the love he had always desired. He recognized what he really needed—the love of

God. What Jesus offered was far greater than anything he currently possessed.

Zacchaeus was prepared to let go of his material wealth in order to gain the friendship of Christ. This is what Jesus meant when he spoke of the kingdom of God: "Again, the kingdom of heaven is like a merchant searching for fine pearls. When he finds a pearl of great price, he goes and sells all that he has and buys it" (Matthew 13:45–46). Zacchaeus found the pearl of great price and was prepared to give up everything to possess it.

From Being Good to Pursuing Holiness

From our earliest instruction we have understood the Christian journey to be about good behavior. This teaching is so prevalent that we have come to believe that simply being good is all that is necessary to get to heaven. We might actually work toward goodness without ever knowing and loving God.

This is not what Jesus intended. He desires that we enter into a relationship with him, as did Zacchaeus, and love others because he first loved us (see 1 John 4:19). In other words, our being good should be the result of an intimate relationship with Jesus, not a replacement for it.

The intentions of the Church's evangelical and catechetical efforts have always been to lead hearts into a transforming relationship with Jesus through the power of the Holy Spirit. It is in this encounter that a heart bound in the grips of selfish sin finds a love worth pursuing. Only this love is capable of convincing us to abandon our selfish and worldly pursuits in order to gain more of the life of Jesus in our hearts.

As our love for Jesus grows, so does our love for others. We begin to see Jesus in others and serve them. This is what Jesus describes in his explanation of the final judgment: "Amen, I say to you, whatever you did for one of these least brothers of mine, you did for me" (Matthew 25:40). As God loves us unconditionally, we naturally begin to see him in other people and desire to love them with the same love we have received.

When we look at the stories of great saints, we see that they all had encounters with the Lord. Mother Teresa encountered Jesus and left her religious community to care for the poor. St. Augustine encountered the Lord, then abandoned his party life to devote his amazing intellect to humanity's understanding of the Lord. St. Clare gave up her wealth and nobility to establish the Poor Clares. St. John Paul II, because of his encounter with Jesus, risked his life during World War II to become a priest.

These saints, living very different lives and possessing different charisms, all had one thing in common: their love for and encounter with Jesus. They all realized that there was something greater than what they were experiencing. They wanted to be part of the family of faith, sons and daughters of "the Father, from whom every family in heaven and on earth is named" (Ephesians 3:14–15).

The Big Picture

My wife and I had just purchased our first home in southern Florida when Hurricane Andrew arose. It was August 24, 1992. Upon hearing of the storm and the expected flooding, we took our daughters and left the neighborhood. The storm, packing 177-mile-per-hour winds, destroyed the entire area. Our neighborhood was so devastated that we did not even recognize it when we returned. Trees and power lines were down, roofs were missing, and new roads had been created around the debris. People were literally walking around dazed as they struggled to take in the destruction.

We found our house and began to sift through the damage. Once we secured the property, we went to each of the neighbors' houses to check on them. There was an elderly couple whose home was safe, but they were running out of food. Fortunately we had stored up a small supply and were able to share what we had with them.

That storm brought about great changes to our little neighborhood. Before the storm it seemed that everyone kept to themselves. Neighbors felt no need to connect with one another. Now people went out and began to care for each other. The storm caused great physical damage to our homes, but it also shocked us back into living as we should. We are not islands unto ourselves but people created to love and be in relationship with others.

Today there are many people who think being a Catholic is more like being a member of a country club than being a child in the family of God. Unfortunately, some believe their role in the Church only involves paying their dues, going to Mass, and trying to be good. They may have no other sense of responsibility toward God, his Church, or other Church members. Despite numerous references in Scripture to the contrary (such as Mark 12:31, "Love your neighbor as yourself"), a common assumption is that the responsibility for building the kingdom and caring for others belongs to priests, religious orders, and lay professionals working for the Church.

Here we see a disconnect between what people do at church and what they do at home. Many profess to be part of the family of God, but they seldom act as if the Church is their family or as if the actual church building is their home.

We need to take it upon ourselves to welcome newcomers to our church. If we don't know people, we should introduce ourselves and let them know that we appreciate their presence at Mass. We should extend invitations to other events that take place in the church. We need to be hospitable hosts who make all who attend feel welcome and wanted. We must restore the paradigm of a loving family within our parishes.

As we grow in our relationship with Jesus, we transition into a new identity. Jesus put it this way: "I no longer call you slaves, because a slave does not know what his master is doing. I have called you friends, because I have told you everything I have heard from my Father" (John 15:15). Jesus is drawing us into a loving union with the Trinity that will enable us, as his adopted siblings, to carry out his mission.

God is our Father; Mother Mary, the spouse of the Holy Spirit, is our mother; and Jesus is our brother. We "received a spirit of adoption, through which we cry, 'Abba, Father!' The Spirit itself bears witness with our spirit that we are children of God, and if children, then heirs, heirs of God and joint heirs with Christ" (Romans 8:15–17). It is precisely by this intimate union that Jesus will unite us to the Father (see John 14:6).

Free to Love

When God made humanity in his image, he gave us the capacity to love as he loves. One of the consequences of sin is that we lost this ability to love God and others as we should. Sin led us to become selfish and self-centered. Even if we want to love God perfectly, we are not capable of such love on our own.

Our focus turns to other things, to fill the void created by the absence of this love. Worldly possessions and passions consume our time and energy. We are bound to the task of providing for ourselves. Caught up in this tunnel vision, we have little to no time to contribute to the needs of others.

This state of disorder is a major obstacle in the pursuit of God and his love. However, our compassionate God will never abandon us to a life devoid of his love.

God sent his only Son into the world to be a model of authentic love. Jesus was selfless and full of compassion as he tended to the needs of all those who came to him. He not only saw but entered into the pain and suffering of his brothers and sisters. His sole desire was to heal them of their brokenness and sin. This was the motivation that led him to suffer, to lay down his life, for the entire world. His life and love culminated in the greatest expression of love known to man: the cross! He was determined to not only save us but also restore our capacity to love.

The truth and reality of the cross changed everything for me. Upon realizing that Jesus died not only for the world but also specifically for me, I opened my heart and invited him to dwell within. As his love flowed into my heart, the God-shaped void began to disappear. His love ministered to the broken areas of my life. Where I once felt insecure and insufficient, I now found security and acceptance.

The love he poured into my heart was so captivating that I desired more. He placed before me a simple invitation: "Take my yoke upon you and learn from me, for I am meek and humble of heart; and you will find rest for yourselves. For my yoke is easy, and my burden light" (Matthew 11:29–30).

I saw my life in a brand new way. I could offer myself to God, who was prepared to meet my every need, or I could continue to live for my passions. The selfless cross stood in stark contrast to the selfishness of the world. I chose the love from the cross!

Embracing the Lord in authentic faith is the key that unlocks the bonds of sin and selfishness. As we give ourselves completely to Jesus, he supplies our every need. The more we are satisfied by Christ's life in us, the less we need from the world, and the freer we are to care for others. Jesus taught his disciples this principle, "You will know the truth, and the truth will set you free" (John 8:32). Our hearts were created to love in this way.

The apostles and other early disciples experienced the freedom and joy that come from focusing on the needs of others instead of oneself:

> All who believed were together and had all things in common; they would sell their property and possessions and divide them among all according to each one's need. Every day they devoted themselves to meeting together in the temple area and to breaking bread in their homes. They ate their meals with exultation and sincerity of heart, praising God and enjoying favor with all the people. (Acts 2:44–47)

If we are going to be authentic disciples of Christ, we must recognize that growing closer to God includes growing closer to others. This may be a struggle at first, because we are accustomed to taking care of only ourselves. As we learn to hear the Spirit's call, he will lead us to serve others.

This service will transform our lives from self-centered concern to other-centered love. Our donation of love for Jesus will unite with his love and be shared with those around us. In this union we become the body of Christ, sacrificed for the world. We become a people of love freely given.

CHAPTER ELEVEN

Evangelization: The Time Is Now
• Deacon Ralph •

The woman left her water jar and went into the town and said to the people, "Come see a man who told me every-thing I have done. Could he possibly be the Messiah?" (John 4:28–29)

Despite the fact that the fathers of Vatican II addressed the topic of evangelization over fifty years ago, many Catholics seem to be only recently hearing about it. And my experience with Catholics around the country leads me to believe that there is no clear and concise understanding of the term *evangelization*. Many admit that this is not what they see themselves participating in but rather what Protestants do. Others have no real understanding of what evangelization involves.

What Is Evangelization?
There are many ways to define evangelization, depending on the context. Here we will focus on a narrow understanding as our working definition. Simply put, evangelization is the process by which one who has a relationship with Jesus Christ leads another to encounter God or establish his or her own relationship with God. So what does it look like when a person is evangelized?

One of the first encounters I had with God was an incredible personal experience. I sensed the Holy Spirit entering my head, flowing down to my toes and back up again, leaving me feeling as if a huge weight had been lifted. God's love stirred my heart in a way I had never before experienced. I suddenly had a tremendous desire to love him back.

A hunger to learn more about the Lord caught me off guard. As I began reading the Scriptures, it was difficult to put them down. The encounter with God changed me; it transformed me.

A few weeks later I was at soccer practice, and one of my best friends came up to me and asked what was going on. He noticed something different about me, but he could not put his finger on it. He said that there was a peace about me that he had never seen before. It was not weird or strange, just different.

After practice I shared with him my encounter with Jesus. His response was typical for that time: "Aw, man, are you becoming a Jesus freak?"

I responded, "If having a relationship with a man who loves me so much that he would die for me makes me a freak, then I guess I am." Within the next year my friend too became a "Jesus freak."

Jesus told the apostles, "Go…and make disciples of all nations, baptizing them in the name of the Father, and of the Son, and of the Holy Spirit, teaching them to observe all that I have commanded you" (Matthew 28:19–20). The apostles discovered that making disciples required evangelization. Peter boldly addressed the crowds on the Day of Pentecost: "You who are Israelites, hear these words" (Acts 2:22).

The apostles also understood that the process of evangelization was not complete until there was evidence of the life of the Holy Spirit in the hearts of new believers. In Acts chapter 8, Philip returned to Jerusalem after preaching to and baptizing the Samaritans. They had heard, believed, and received baptism, but there was no evidence of the Spirit's presence. This was a problem that required Peter and John to return with Philip to Samaria. Upon laying their hands on the new believers, the Holy Spirit filled the Samaritans with evident power.

The Process of Evangelization

Our Lord's encounter with the woman at the well in John's Gospel is a classic example of evangelization. Anyone who desires to be a disciple of Christ and wants to help others come to know him would be wise to spend time studying this passage. There are several key points:

1. Jesus went to the woman. "He came to a town of Samaria called Sychar…[and] sat down there at the well" (John 4:5, 6).

2. He found a commonality with the woman: Their shared need for water provided the opportunity to engage her in conversation. "Give me a drink" (John 4:7).

3. He engaged her in conversation. Without fear of public opinion, he spoke to one who was rejected by her village. "If you knew the gift of God and who was saying to you, 'Give me a drink,' you would have asked him and he would have given you living water" (John 4:10).

4. He helped her identify a need. Her thirst was not for water but for something greater: love. "Everyone who drinks this water will be thirsty again; but whoever drinks the water I shall give will never thirst; the water I shall give will become in him a spring of water welling up to eternal life" (John 4:13–14).

5. He guided her to understand what her heart really desired. The love of her several husbands was not the kind of love she wanted. "I

know that the Messiah is coming, the one called the Anointed; when he comes, he will tell us everything" (John 4:25).

6. He led her to make a choice: She could remain in her brokenness or journey toward truth and life. "But the hour is coming, and is now here, when true worshipers will worship the Father in Spirit and truth; and indeed the Father seeks such people to worship him. God is Spirit, and those who worship him must worship in Spirit and truth" (John 4:23–24).

7. He blessed the woman with the gifts of faith, hope, and love. While the text does not describe her conversion, we know that the encounter was a profound one, as she left the well and witnessed to the people in the village about Jesus. "Come see a man who told me everything I have done. Could he possibly be the Messiah?" (John 4:29).

The process of evangelization brings about a genuine change in the hearts of those who encounter Jesus. When we encounter him, we too want to go back to the town and tell everyone what happened.

Why would the woman share this good news with the very people who humiliated her? It is evident that when the love of God is given access to our hearts, it heals our wounds, restores our dignity, and gives us the ability to selflessly love. We are simply and fundamentally changed when we meet Jesus.

My Personal Testimony

I was a cradle Catholic, self-defined as part of the "lost generations." Many of those born between the 1960s and the present, myself included, were poorly catechized. I knew so little about my faith that I thought I was a Christian because I was not Jewish. Despite being baptized and confirmed, I had no idea about who Jesus and the Holy

Spirit were. Honestly, the only reason I received the sacraments was to please my parents.

Sadly, once I received the sacrament of confirmation, I left the Church. Religion really did not mean anything to me. I did not encounter God there. I now know he was there, but I could not see him.

For many years I pursued false gods, such as sports. Soccer became my life and reason for being. My success in soccer gave me popularity, confidence, and value as an individual. But eventually I realized that soccer could never fill the real, hidden void within my heart. I was trying to earn the right to be loved by being good at something. I realized that what I wanted was not the popularity or celebrity of a soccer star but the love that I hoped stardom would bring.

The Lord graciously allowed me to see the folly of that pursuit. He brought Christian disciples into my life, who led me to open my heart to Jesus. To this day I am grateful to those who reached out and led me to Jesus.

The greatest person of influence during this time was the girl-friend I mentioned earlier—a beautiful woman named Susan (who later became my wife). She was a faith-filled Catholic who loved the Lord and understood what it really meant to have Jesus in her life. Susan always considered Jesus her boyfriend. It was clear to me that I could never have a relationship with just Susan; Jesus was always going to be a part of any relationship with her. That is exactly what she wanted, but it was not exactly what I wanted. She repeatedly invited me to Mass, and I persistently said no.

When Susan's attempts to bring me to God did not work, she introduced me to a youth group and their leader, a youth minister and evangelist working with Miami Youth for Christ. It was the right time for me to hear a clear presentation of the Gospel. I will never forget the night I gave my life to Christ.

It was a traditional Protestant altar call. The only problem was that I had fallen asleep. When those in the crowd around me stood up, I awoke and also stood. I had no idea what I was doing, but there I was standing with the others.

As instructed, I followed the crowd backstage and was placed in a small group. A counselor came and reviewed the simple Gospel message and invited us to pray. I prayed, "Jesus, I do not really know you, but if you are real, I want you in my life."

After a quick mental test to see if I was really serious about my prayer, I knew and felt God's presence and peace. It did not make sense: I had just given myself to someone, yet I felt so free. Can you really be free if you give yourself to Jesus? Yes. "You will know the truth, and the truth will set you free" (John 8:32).

You see, we are not asking God to be part of *our* lives; we are really asking to be part of *his* life. We give ourselves to Jesus because he first gave his life to us (see 1 John 4:19). When we make this decision of faith, we begin a process of learning how to give God every part of our lives.

This was difficult for me, because I was accustomed to living according to my rules and desires. Now I had to obey God's will and deal with my sinful habits. I am still in the midst of the battle. Every day I learn how to die to myself, to my desires for pleasures and worldly materials. And the Holy Spirit has been with me every step of the way, encouraging, convicting, and consoling me.

Sharing the Gospel

It has always been the mission of the Church to share Christ and his message with the world. The world is starving to know the truth about God and how to find him. Many people see crosses in homes and churches, on jewelry and billboards, but do not understand how a cross is applicable to their lives. What does it mean that Jesus died on the cross for us?

Our mission is to help others understand just what Jesus's death and resurrection mean. This can be shared in four simple points:

1. You were created to be in relationship with a God who loves you unconditionally (see Genesis 1:26; Psalm 139).

2. Sin (original and your own) breaks your relationship with our loving God (Genesis 3:8).

3. Jesus died on the cross to pay the debt for our sins (John 3:16).

4. You must decide whether you want to return to a relationship with God as his child or remain separated from him (Deuteronomy 30:15; 2 Peter 3:9).

The Gospel of Jesus Christ is relevant to every human being. The challenge of evangelization is to demonstrate how our encounter with Jesus has made a difference in our life. This is called giving witness or testimony.

For many Catholics, learning how to share their personal testimony was not a part of their formation. Everywhere I travel I find that the majority of Catholics prefer to keep their faith in Jesus private. But the "Great Commission" of Matthew 28 does not ask us to do something. Jesus did not say, "If you feel comfortable," or "If you want to, share the Gospel." He said, Go and share the good news of the Gospel. It is essential that every disciple of Jesus know and share the Gospel.

A good way to start is by sharing about our own encounters with the Lord. We can do this by answering one simple question: "What has the Lord done in our life?" Answering this question requires us to reveal portions of our spiritual life to others. This can be quite challenging, because we are not accustomed to talking about what God is doing with us. However, we need to become comfortable doing it.

When I was a youth minister, I often led retreats for teens. At the conclusion of a retreat, I would ask the teens about their experience of it. They would say it was awesome or they loved it. As I pressed them to explain why, they fumbled with their thoughts and words, unable to give a clear, articulate reason why they loved the retreat.

I thought this was a typical teen lack-of-maturity issue. However, when I tried to get adults to do the same at their retreat, they also were hard pressed to clearly explain what God had done for them.

We have grown to be very guarded, and sharing deeply personal information is rare. Perhaps we are afraid of what other people will think of us when we talk about what Jesus has done in our lives. Consider this: The enemy uses this fear to prevent us from showing the world that Jesus is alive.

It is important for people to see that a relationship with Jesus is possible and that it can be a lively, joyful relationship. By developing a personal testimony, we are able to help other people come to know Jesus.

The Lord's perfect love casts out all fear (see 1 John 4:18). So ask the Holy Spirit to take away your fear and help you share your faith with others. Jesus promised, "The Advocate, the Holy Spirit that the Father will send in my name—he will teach you everything and remind you of all that [I] told you" (John 14:26).

There are three basic elements to your testimony, and I think you are able to see each of them in my personal testimony.

1. What were you like before you encountered Christ? What was your religious background? What did you think about God? What did you think about life and its meaning?

I was a poorly formed cradle Catholic who did not believe in Jesus. I pursued the pleasure of the world and sought after fame. I was selfish and did not think I needed God.

2. How did you encounter Jesus? Who told you about Jesus? What were the circumstances that helped you come to realize that God was real and that he loved you?

I encountered Christ as a result of Susan's introducing me to my youth minister, who invited me to a Youth for Christ Rally. At that rally I experienced God's love for me and my call to be a disciple.

3. How has your life changed since you started living with and for Jesus? What concrete impact has your relationship with Christ had on you?

I experienced a hunger to grow closer to Jesus. I began to pray and read the Scriptures. I also realized that soccer was not going to be able to fulfill me; only God could fill the void in my heart.

People need to see in our testimonies what it looks like to have a relationship with God. We should give an honest portrayal of the joys and struggles that disciples experience when following Jesus. People need to see in us the fruit of what living with Jesus can bring. Our joy, peace, and happiness need to be visible. We cannot keep them to ourselves!

When others see changes happening in our lives, they may want to take a look at their own lives. They may wonder if they too can experience the joy that we have. An encounter with us might provoke questions. Welcome these as possible openings of the door to faith.

Go! Tell!

If those who have encountered the Lord never talk about him, then how will others come to know his love? If God's own children do not reveal our Father God, then who will?

> But how can they call on him in whom they have not believed? And how can they believe in him of whom they have not heard? And how can they hear without someone to preach?… Thus faith comes from what is heard, and what is heard comes through the word of Christ. (Romans 10:14, 17)

Evangelization is part of our responsibility in the family of God. As a child of God, you are called to share in the mission of Jesus Christ by witnessing to the truth of his existence. Putting yourself in situations where you can share God's love allows you to exercise your faith. This will sustain you and empower you to be a light for the world.

Do not let fear prevent you from being God's witness. "Do not fear. Take courage" (Deuteronomy 31:6; Isaiah 41:10; 54:4; Matthew 9:2; John 16:33). You can do this! You really can "go out to all the world and tell the good news."[7]

CHAPTER TWELVE

Discipleship: It's for Everyone

• Deacon Ralph •

In those days he departed to the mountain to pray, and he spent the night in prayer to God. When day came, he called his disciples to himself, and from them he chose Twelve, whom he also named apostles: Simon, whom he named Peter, and his brother Andrew, James, John, Philip, Bartholomew, Matthew, Thomas, James the son of Alphaeus, Simon who was called a Zealot, and Judas the son of James, and Judas Iscariot, who became a traitor. (Luke 6:12–16)

Imagine you were one of the original twelve apostles, handpicked by Jesus. The apostles had been following Jesus ever since he called them by name, and now they were selected to form an elite group. Apart from feeling honored, they probably wondered why he needed to create a smaller group of disciples.

Jesus had a specific purpose in mind for the apostles, and in time they would come to understand what that was. They would see it was not a position of honor but an important role in the saving plan of God. They would be responsible for forming what is now known as the Catholic Church.

After Jesus's ascension to heaven, at the Feast of Pentecost, the Holy Spirit empowered these men to take on the mission of Jesus Christ, to "go and make disciples" (Matthew 28:19). Who could be better suited to make disciples than those who had been taught by Christ? The apostles' intimate relationship with Jesus, developed over three years, had convinced them of his true identity as God. The Holy Spirit's arrival at Pentecost confirmed beyond any doubt that Jesus was the Christ. They chose to give their very lives in service to his kingdom.

Three thousand people were added to the number on the Day of Pentecost (Acts 2:41) but had no idea what it meant to be Jesus's disciple. How were they to live now? Would they continue living according to the Law? What about Jesus's teachings that seemed to contradict the Law?

In the same way that God used Abraham and the patriarchs as living examples of authentic faith, Jesus intended to use his apostles to model authentic discipleship through relational ministry. The apostles used their personal experience, their knowledge, and the guidance of the Holy Spirit to lead others to follow Christ.

St. Paul later described this process: "Be imitators of me, as I am of Christ" (1 Corinthians 11:1). He understood his role as a disciple to be one who lives like Christ. In every circumstance a disciple must strive to think like Christ, respond like Christ, and conduct himself or herself as a representative of Christ. Each disciple is called to be a living example for others.

Back to the Basics

The apostles understood that making a disciple involved two steps:

Step one: Evangelize them. People had to be led to encounter Christ through the Holy Spirit.

Step two: Train them to become disciples. The apostles had to teach new Christians how to develop their faith, equipping them with knowledge of Christ's teachings and guiding them to live in the Spirit.

Acts chapter 2 records what the early Church did to anchor their new converts in the faith. "They devoted themselves to the teaching of the apostles and to the communal life, to the breaking of the bread and to the prayers" (Acts 2:42). These four disciplines were essential to the early Church and are still essential today. They are the four fundamental disciplines for every disciple of Christ.

I use the word *fundamental* because I want to emphasize that these are not special devotions but critical components of the life of a disciple. Every disciple must engage in prayer, study, fellowship, and the Eucharist in order to maintain and nourish a relationship with Christ.

Daily Prayer

In high school my youth minister took me under his wing and began to form me into a disciple of Jesus. To develop the spiritual discipline of daily prayer, he instructed me to do the following:

Select a consistent time of day to pray.

Create a place to pray in my room or home.

Religious orders have strong formation in this particular discipline. They gather together for communal prayers, and when not working or eating, members return to their cells (bedrooms) to pray on their own. Personal prayer must be at the core of a disciple's relationship with Jesus.

When I first started to pray, I decided to pray for fifteen minutes every day. I thought that this was going to be easy, but I came to realize that creating a habit (virtue) of prayer was actually a very difficult battle. It was not enough to give Jesus my list of requests; I needed to learn how to listen to him.

Although sitting in silence was agonizingly difficult, I stuck to it and gradually grew to enjoy it. In the process of being still, I learned how to hear God. It was like tuning in to a radio station on an old dial radio: It took a while to find the station, but when I got it right, there was no static—just crisp, clear sound.

Scripture Study: The Apostles' Teaching

In addition to prayer, my youth minister encouraged me to read the Bible. He gave me a brief walk through the Scriptures and selected Mark's Gospel for me to read. I was not an avid reader by any stretch of the imagination, so the (short) book of Mark was the perfect way to introduce me to the Word of God. Much to my surprise, when I finished reading Mark, I was craving more.

My youth minister also spent time teaching me about the role of the Holy Spirit in my life. He instructed me to invite the Spirit to lead me in my reading, prayer, and study of Scripture. Every time I sat down to pray or to study Scripture, I was to invite the Holy Spirit to be present, not as an observer but as an instructor. "Speak, LORD, for your servant is listening" (1 Samuel 3:9).

The power of reading Scripture is in the application. It is not enough to simply read the stories. Hebrews tells us that Scripture is "living and effective" (Hebrews 4:12). The Bible is clearly like no other book ever written. It is God's Word, divinely inspired, and there is the potential for an encounter with God anytime we read it.

God speaks to us through Scripture, often addressing the problems we face and our current situations. In addition to looking for such applications, we do well to ask the Holy Spirit to reveal how he wants us to apply what we are reading. Our constant question while we read Scripture must be, "How does this apply to my life?"

The Breaking of the Bread: The Mass

The breaking of the bread, the Mass, was my least favorite of the four disciplines of a disciple. My experience of the Mass up to that point had been uneventful. I saw little value in the rituals and movements because I did not understand them. Although I had some amazing religious education teachers, I had not been very open to their instruction.

I knew the Church believed that the Eucharist was actually the Body and Blood of Christ, but I did not believe that. For many years I had processed through the Communion line, responding "Amen" when the minister said, "The Body of Christ." I was not actually responding, "Amen, I believe," only going through the motions.

When I was twenty-five years old and serving as a youth minister in my parish, my pastor wanted me to become a Eucharistic minister. I would be required to stand in front of each person, hold up the Eucharist, and declare, "The Body of Christ." It was evident that this invitation to become a Eucharistic minister was also the Lord's call to a deeper understanding of his presence in the Mass.

For the next three months I studied the Church's teaching on the Eucharist. I spent a particularly long time contemplating what it meant for the priest to ask the Holy Spirit to transform the bread and wine into the Body, Blood, soul, and divinity of Christ. This time was fruitful. I gained a deeper understanding and finally felt free to choose to believe.

I was amazed at the realization that I had merely been going through the motions when I received Communion. What a tremendous joy to discover that the Lord had been so patient with me. He was continually present in the Eucharist despite my unbelief. He was waiting for me!

Fellowship

Six months after my conversion, it was clear that I was growing spiritually. My youth minister encouraged me to establish a small group of men with whom I could share and grow. I prayed and invited five other young men to join me in this faith-sharing group.

Our youth group met every Friday night at six, and we decided to come an hour early for our small group meeting. We were serious about taking care of each other's spiritual lives, so we required everyone to be committed. We established a rule that if someone could not be there, he had to contact one of the other guys. If he did not inform someone, we would go get him.

Our purpose was to grow in our faith by honestly sharing our journey with each other. During these meetings we shared both victories and struggles. It was important to share not only the good things but also our difficulties with sin and obedience.

One day one of the guys did not come to the group. He had not contacted any of us ahead of time, so as promised, we decided to go and get him. We all jumped into my car and drove to his house. We knocked, and he finally opened the door.

"Dude, you're missing our group."

He tried to make a cheap excuse, but we saw through it and lovingly hauled him into the car. Within ten minutes he shared how he had fallen into sin and was afraid to face us. It was a very powerful moment for all of us. The accountability we shared was affecting our lives.

Seeing his pain and need for healing, we got back into my car, drove to the church rectory, and rang the doorbell. Father opened the door and was surprised to find six young men standing on the porch. I apologized for disturbing him at home and explained that our friend really needed him.

The other guys and I went back to the car and prayed for our friend while he was in confession. After a few minutes it was clear that the Holy Spirit had been alive and active in this situation. Our friend came bounding to the car, looking as if the weight of the world had been lifted off his shoulders.

God desires all of his children to journey into a new life of faith in him. This requires a disciple not only to learn about God but also to trust in him. When we gather for catechesis, Bible study, or other faith sharing, we must go beyond learning information. It is critical that we not only share knowledge about God but also personalize it. We need to share the struggles that accompany the life of faith. This fosters faith-centered accountability that facilitates trust in God, which helps transform us into true disciples.

Now, many people enter sharing groups hoping to grow in the Lord but are hesitant to disclose their own personal struggles. Conversations remain superficial. People may talk about what they are learning but not offer personal feelings or issues. Fear keeps them protectively silent and shallow.

Small groups need to be safe places where people are free to share what is really going on in their lives. Mature disciples should run these groups and establish standards for sharing on a personal level. This provides a model for others to follow.

The group becomes a practice ground for applying what has been learned. Sharing one's struggles takes faith and trust. Responding to one another's struggles takes love. Thus the group exercises the very virtues in which the members seek to grow.

My Training in Discipleship

My journey into discipleship began my senior year of high school. The Lord had created the perfect circumstances for what some might call my chance meeting with him, surrounding me with several disciples. My youth minister had been reaching out to me for six months prior to the encounter that really changed me. It was clear that he cared about me and my faith, as he made a tremendous effort to get to know me as a person. After my initial conversion, he was the obvious choice to help guide me in discipleship.

When I shared with him that I had given my life to the Lord, I was shocked by his reaction. I expected him to be excited, but instead he simply said, "Did ya?" Experience had taught him to wait and see if my decision to follow the Lord would last. He was cool and calm, quietly challenging me to prove my resolve.

After all of his personal investment, his response was so emotionless. I was confused. Is this not what he wanted?

A few days later he asked me if I was still serious about my decision to follow Christ. I answered with a very emphatic yes! He then challenged me to enter into a training process. He suggested I meet with him weekly to discuss how to establish the four fundamental spiritual disciplines in my life—prayer, the apostles' teaching, the breaking of the bread, and fellowship.

It did not take long for me to fall back into my undisciplined routine. Fortunately, my youth minister was equally quick to chide me for slacking off. Over the next two years, under his watchful eye, I developed the discipline needed to walk on my own. When the time came for me to go away to college, I was grounded enough in my disciplines to maintain them by myself.

Discipleship training cannot be just an afterthought. It must be a very specific and intentional process. St. Paul gives us an excellent example in his training of Timothy. In the book of Acts and in his letters to Timothy, we see how Paul prepared him to take on a pastoral role in the life of the Church.

As part of his training, Timothy served with Paul in his ministry. At the appointed time Paul left him in charge of the Church in Ephesus, knowing that his work with Timothy was complete. Timothy went on to train others to be disciples. It is important to point out that each of us, by virtue of baptism, is also called to make disciples.

While speaking at a conference, I asked those present to raise their hands if they were disciples of Jesus. I followed up with two other questions: "If you are a disciple of Jesus Christ, then tell me, who are your current disciples? Whom are you training to become a disciple of Jesus?"

I watched their eyes and noticed a curious look as they struggled to understand the questions. They either were not certain of the meaning of my questions or were unaware that training new disciples was part of their job.

A disciple of Jesus is always called to make new disciples. If we are going to fulfill our mission as disciples, we must become deliberate in that effort.

Intentional Discipleship Training

Successful training of new disciples to live in the power of God requires very intentional formation. We need a proper vision, a specific goal, and a plan to achieve the goal. The vision needs to be clearly understood by all involved in the process; this includes the trainers as well as the new disciples. The plan must be actionable and measurable. Throughout the process we must evaluate the effectiveness of our plan, identify problems, and make necessary adjustments. Discipleship is not going to magically happen; it will take work.

This process comes at a great price. We must be actively engaged in personal evangelization and discipleship, using the teaching magisterium as both a guide for instruction and a guard against poor teaching. We cannot leave this to the clergy, lay professionals, and programs. Everyone who desires to belong to the kingdom of God must work toward the building of the kingdom.

Each of us should begin by determining where we are weak in our own disciplines and seek the Spirit's help in growing and developing those. As we work on these disciplines, we may also seek good methods of personal evangelization and discipleship formation. As we dispose ourselves to God's work, the Spirit will take notice. And when we are ready, he will place people in our path who need our help.

Get ready. There is much to be done.

CHAPTER THIRTEEN

Called to the Feast

• *Fr. Dave* •

And it happened that, while he was with them at table, he took bread, said the blessing, broke it, and gave it to them. With that their eyes were opened and they recognized him, but he vanished from their sight. Then they said to each other, "Were not our hearts burning [within us] while he spoke to us on the way and opened the scriptures to us?" So they set out at once and returned to Jerusalem where they found gathered together the eleven and those with them who were saying, "The Lord has truly been raised and has appeared to Simon!" Then the two recounted what had taken place on the way and how he was made known to them in the breaking of the bread. (Luke 24:30–35)

⚜Were not our hearts burning?

Doesn't it seem kind of odd that the disciples were walking with Jesus on the road and didn't recognize him? Well, maybe not if we keep in mind that Jesus had been dead twenty-four hours earlier. It's pretty safe to assume these disciples were not expecting to run into Jesus on their short walk to Emmaus. They were in his presence yet did not recognize him until he broke the bread.

Are we any different?

Jesus is constantly in our midst, but do we see him? He is present to us and speaks to us at every liturgy. Do our hearts burn? Do we encounter him in the breaking of the bread?

I'm certain that every time you go to Mass, you have an amazing, heart-burning, life-changing experience of God. Right?

You're saying this is not always your experience? Okay, perhaps not always, but most of the time? Sometimes? Once? Ever?

Sunday's Encounter

For a large percentage of Catholics, the only time put aside for God is Sunday Mass. And oftentimes their experience of Sunday Mass is less than prayerful and heart-burning. There are a million reasons why this may be the case.

One mom said to me, "You can't imagine how frustrating it can be getting my kids ready for Mass in the morning. By the time I walk into the church, I am already at the boiling point." Going to Mass is not supposed to be a near occasion of sin, but I get it. I know that it can be difficult.

The Mass may not seem to impact us the way we would like or know that it should. Perhaps the music or the preaching is not the style we prefer. Maybe the sacred space is not so sacred; maybe the church resembles a ski lodge. Who has never said something like, "I would get more out of the Mass if the music were different, if Father would slow down, if Father would speed up, if the child behind me or spouse beside me were better behaved," and on and on and on?

Probably everyone has been distracted, preoccupied, or otherwise engaged during Mass at one time or another. Perhaps we can't get our mind off the playoff game that starts forty-five minutes after Mass. If we are honest, the prayer of our heart is that we are able to get out of the parking lot as quickly as heavenly possible.

While we can hope for and perhaps work for change, the greatest change that has to take place is in us. It is in our hearts.

Don't get me wrong. Music, preaching, and environment all matter. But nothing affects your encounter with God more than the heart you bring to worship. Nothing. If we are to encounter Jesus more personally and profoundly in the Mass, our hearts must change.

Sadly, when hearts do not change, people give up. Some get so frustrated with the whole experience that they stop attending Mass. This is not the answer to our frustrations.

People sometimes tell me why they stop attending Mass. "I'm too busy; the kids have other places they need to be; Sunday is my only day to relax; I'm too tired; there is never enough parking; I don't feel worthy; I don't want to be a hypocrite…" I think you get the point. But I have to say that the most common reason I hear from people is that they simply don't get anything out of going to Mass. The translation here is: They don't encounter God.

For many Catholics, Mass has become a lifeless, ritualistic routine with no real personal meaning and little relevance to the rest of their lives. In some ways this is a childish response. By saying, "I don't get anything out of it," people are essentially saying, "It's all about me." Don't get me wrong, the liturgy is partly about us.

Once I heard an individual say, "You are not supposed to get anything out of the Mass; you are supposed to give yourself to the Mass." I don't agree with this. We are supposed to get something out of Mass, and we are also supposed to give something. This second point is where we often fall short. We don't really give ourselves to the liturgy. We don't fully engage our intellects or our hearts. Oftentimes, if we are honest, we just show up.

In the end, we get what we give, which is often very little. It's sad too, because the reality is that every time we go to Mass, there is the possibility of a life-altering experience. That is not some pious statement but a fact. More times than I can remember, people have shared with me about significant encounters with Christ that took place within the liturgy. And their hearts were changed by those encounters.

So Why Go?

Perhaps a good starting place is to ask the simple question, "Why do I go to Mass?"

Because God said so.

Well, that pretty much settles it.

For some, maybe, while for others perhaps not.

It is important to remember that the Lord commands us to make his day holy. It is one of the Ten Commandments, so it can't be taken lightly. Your Sunday should look different from the other days of the week, and football and no work are not the differences for which the Lord is looking. The Lord invites us to put this time aside for him. We are to stop, reflect, pray, give and receive, and offer thanks—in a word, to worship. If we think about the amount of time we spend doing lots of worthless other things, is spending about an hour with God in Mass too much to ask?

And lest we forget, Mass on Sundays is an obligation for Catholics. Sometimes we don't like that word *obligation*, and when we hear it we want to rebel or resist. Let's keep in mind that life is full of obligations. Do you feel obliged to see that your children are fed? Are you obliged to go to work? Is your insurance premium optional?

Going to Mass on Sunday is so much more than meeting an obligation, but that is a part of it. Hopefully this is not the only reason you attend, but even if it is, there is virtue in that. Many parents expect "Because I said so" to be met without question. Perhaps every now and then we can give the Lord the same due. In the end, to say we responded to the Lord's obligation is not such a bad thing.

My relationship with the Mass (yes, I have a relationship with the Mass, because in the Mass I experience Jesus) is similar to Tarzan's seemingly reckless but very precise swinging from vine to vine through the jungles of Africa. He grabs a vine while falling from a tree, then like a pendulum arches up again in search of the next vine. As he reaches out for that next vine, he lets go of the first. If he lets go too early, he will fall to the floor of the jungle, hopefully to be rescued by Jane.

Forgive the simple analogy, but the Eucharist is like that for me. Each day I receive Jesus in the Mass, and this nourishes me, propels me to the next day, when I reach out once again to receive Jesus in the Mass. If he were not there—were I to "miss the vine"—I would surely fall. If I am going to really live the abundant life Christ has for me, I must receive him in the Eucharist. "Unless you eat the flesh of the Son of Man and drink his blood, you do not have life within you" (John 6:53).

One of the great things about the Mass is the many opportunities it presents to encounter Jesus. It is not an all or nothing experience. The Mass is made up of several parts, and Christ can be encountered in many and various ways. If for whatever reason we totally zone out during the penitential act or the readings, all is not lost.

The Church has taught that Christ is present in the Mass in four primary ways:

in the community gathered
in the Word of God proclaimed

in the priest presiding

in the Eucharist, his Body and Blood[8]

Let's look at each of these.

The Community

Jesus promised that wherever two or more gather in his name, he will be in their midst (see Matthew 18:20). At the start of every Mass, we make the Sign of the Cross and say, "In the name of the Father and of the Son and of the Holy Spirit." This is not merely a gesture that signals the beginning of something, like a coin toss at a football game. Rather it is a statement of faith and fact. We are gathered in the name of and in the presence of the Trinity. We are gathered in Jesus; he is present in the community gathered.

When Jesus became flesh, he forever united all of humanity with God. Saints and sinners; black, brown, and white; male and female; young and old; rich and poor—all people are taken up in Christ. I always enjoy being at parishes that have a rich diversity of people gathered from various ethnic, socioeconomic, and cultural backgrounds. In that diversity I see the beauty of God's all-encompassing reach and call.

If that is the case, how can we fail to encounter him?

Perhaps we see as man sees and not as God sees (see 1 Samuel 16:7). Maybe *you* see old Mrs. Grouch-a-Lot, who eight years ago complained that your baby had the nerve to cry during Mass. God may see a fragile, elderly widow who is lonely and hurting.

Or maybe *you* see Mr. What's-He-Doing-Here? Everyone knows he made a lot of money on questionable financial dealings. Perhaps God sees someone trying his best to do what is right and the anonymous donor for the new playground for the school.

And every good Catholic sees the Christmas and Easter family, who have the gall to take their pew for these special feasts. Who knows exactly what God sees? Maybe a family making their first step back to him, wondering how they will be welcomed.

What is important to remember is that we are on this faith journey together. And we can see this when we go to Mass. A mystery of our faith is that the Church is both holy and scandalous; she is full of saints and sinners. There is probably no clearer place to see this than among the community gathered at Mass (with maybe the exception of looking at oneself in a mirror).

It has been said that if we could see one another as God sees us, then we would be tempted to bow down and worship.[9] Such is the dignity of every human person. This is what God sees when he gazes on the community gathered for Mass every Sunday morning. Is it what you see?

We have the opportunity every time we attend Mass to encounter Christ in our brothers and sisters. It's important that we pray for eyes that can see Jesus in parishioners who are bruised, broken, and in radical need of God. This is the population that Jesus invited (Mark 2:17). In that we are no different. We all come to Mass in need of God's healing mercy. How can we be surprised or frustrated at the person in the pew in front of us?

Jesus, help us see as you see.

The Word

Catholics believe that Jesus is present in the Word of God. I saw this most splendidly celebrated in Kenya, Africa.

The second reading had been completed, and the congregation began singing the Alleluia. Down the aisle processed—well, danced is probably a better description—the deacon with eight or ten other parishioners. The deacon was carrying the book of the Gospels. Another person had incense, a couple had candles, while several others had beautiful arrays of fresh flowers. Everyone sang and clapped as if they were welcoming a king, which in fact they were.

It was a beautiful experience. I was struck with the feeling, "They get it! They understand what's going on here and are celebrating the Lord's presence."

In every liturgy the Word of God is proclaimed. But how often do we zone out?

One of the reasons we may do so is that we don't experience a personal connection to the Word. We have heard some of the readings a hundred times but don't connect them to our own life experience. Hopefully the homily will help with that. But even if it doesn't, we can still get something out of the readings. Here are a couple of suggestions to help us do that.

A great exercise is to look through the readings before Mass; read them at home before you leave for church or maybe in the car with the family on the way to Mass (provided, of course, you are not driving). It's kind of like priming the pump of your soul. Some reflection before Mass enables us to be more present to the Word of God during the liturgy.

Another simple thing you can do is remind yourself before the readings that God wants you to hear something. Then listen for what that may be. "Jesus, what are you saying to me through today's readings?" is a good prayer.

Finally, imagine what you would preach about if you were responsible for giving the homily. That should keep things interesting.

I recall a time when I was preaching about the power of God's Word to change our lives. At the end of Mass an elderly woman approached me and asked if I wanted to hear about the time when the Lord changed her life. She went on to tell me:

> A few years ago my husband and I went to the 7:30 A.M. Mass, as we did every week. The Gospel that day was the story about the woman at the well [John 4], and I know I had heard it dozens of times before. But, Father, for some reason that morning it was different. As I was listening to the Gospel, I felt like my heart was going to burst. My soul was screaming, "I want that living water."
>
> I just knew that there was living water that I had yet to taste. Ever since hearing that Gospel, I have longed for the living water of which Jesus spoke, and he continues to give it to me.

This lady had encountered Jesus in the Word of God, and it changed her.

We really can't say that God never speaks to us; he speaks to us every time we go to Mass. The real question is, are we listening?

The Priest

Again, we see as man sees.

As a way of honoring priests, some cultures have the custom of kissing a priest's hands. I have to admit that, when I first experienced this, it caused me to be a little uncomfortable. And at times it still does. I am aware that the custom is not about me but about what I represent, but it is still a humbling experience.

Ultimately the priest is an icon of Christ. He reveals this most clearly in offering the sacrifice of the Mass. The priest participates uniquely in Christ's perfect and eternal offering to the Father. The priest is called to lead the congregation to the very heart of the Father. This too is humbling.

There is nothing that the priest has done to make himself worthy of serving at the altar. Christ's presence in him is not determined by his personal holiness or his skill in preaching. Rather it comes from the gift of ordination. It is only by the grace of God that the priest is able to be a priest and do what he does. At times it takes eyes of faith to see this.

While the priest represents Christ in a particular manner during the liturgy, this does not mean that he is without fault in his personal life. He is every bit as human as any other member of the parish community. He has many of the same fears, struggles, temptations, hopes, and dreams as you. He has personality traits you like and perhaps ones that drive you crazy. You may one day love the homily he preaches at Mass and another day can't wait for him to sit down.

This makes the fact that the priest reveals Christ even more notable. It is God's grace that enables you to see Christ in an imperfect person presiding at every Mass. Pray for this grace, that you may encounter Jesus in your priest.

Look beyond the Bread

When we speak of the real presence of Christ in the Eucharistic elements, it is not to say that he is not really present in the other ways. Rather we are highlighting his unique, singular presence in the Eucharist. Christ is really present—Body, Blood, soul, and divinity— in what looks like bread and wine. This perhaps requires the greatest eyes of faith.

How can this be? You are not the first to ask such a question.

In the sixth chapter of John's Gospel, Jesus says that he is the living bread come down from heaven. He affirms that his flesh is real food and his blood real drink. As you know, some of his followers could not accept this teaching. "This saying is hard; who can accept it?" (John 6:60). In fact, they could no longer follow Jesus. Note that Jesus didn't back down. He did not call them back to explain that he did not mean it literally but only symbolically. No, Jesus allowed them to leave; he watched them walk away.

At the Last Supper Jesus took bread and said, "This is my body" (see Matthew 26:26). He did not say *this bread* is my body, only *this* is my body. At the consecration at each and every Mass, when the priest, in the power of the Holy Spirit, prays the words of consecration over the bread and wine, they cease to exist. The bread and wine are changed, transformed into the Body and Blood of Christ.

Jesus is not in the bread, because there is no longer bread; all that remains is Jesus. To believe this requires faith, and we need to ask the Lord for this faith. While what we hold in our hands looks and tastes like bread, and what we put to our lips is sweet like wine, the essence, what it is, has changed: It is Jesus. At times our prayer is that of the father who asked Jesus to heal his son: "I do believe, help my unbelief!" (Mark 9:24).

We consume the Eucharist because we need food for the journey. There is no way we can be faithful to God and live the abundant life he has invited us to without his help and grace. This we experience most powerfully in the reception of Jesus in the Eucharist. The moments after receiving the Eucharist are a sacred time. Let your spirit echo the words of Elizabeth, "And how does this happen to me, that…my Lord should come to me?" (see Luke 1:43). Amazingly he comes; he comes to us.

The Hits Keep on Coming

While the Church teaches that Christ is primarily present in the four ways addressed (the community gathered, the Word of God, the priest, and the Eucharistic elements), this does not mean that these are the only places we can encounter Christ. Hardly. I suppose the list is almost endless, but it may be beneficial to name a few other ways we may encounter Christ in the Mass.

God shows himself in the music of the liturgy. Music in the liturgy is not merely a filler, something that moves us from point A to point B. Rather it can reveal God to hearts and minds that are open to receive. Such is the power of music.

I am aware that different people have varying tastes regarding music. There are some songs that stir my heart and help make me more receptive to the Lord's grace. Hopefully you hear music at Mass that draws you closer to God.

Personally, one of the most moving parts of the Mass is the penitential act. I understand why we have it at the beginning of the Mass, but sometimes I wish it were later. I often get the sense that we are not quite ready for it. We have just arrived and are hardly settled in the pew when we begin the penitential act. I'm afraid this often doesn't get the attention it deserves.

We begin the Mass in this way so that we can be free of our sin and enter more worthily into the rest of the liturgy. If entered with serious intention, the penitential act can be a wonderful experience of God's mercy. How seriously do we take that moment?

Let's be honest. Is it, "Lord, please show me my sin, so that I may know your mercy in this Mass"? Or, "Is that vestment Father is wearing really pink? He looks like a six-foot bottle of Pepto-Bismol."

The liturgy is full of opportunities to experience the Lord and his love for us. I continually pray that God will open my mind and heart so as to receive more of his grace in the liturgy. I pray that he will heal my blindness so that I am able to see him. I ask him to change my heart.

Thanks a Lot

Have you ever been extremely grateful to someone and not known how to properly say thank you? I'm talking gratitude so great that a box of chocolates or a bouquet of flowers just isn't going to do it.

A number of years ago my father had quadruple-bypass heart surgery. Speaking to the surgeon after the procedure, I was struck by the fact that, just moments earlier, this physician had my father's heart in his hands. "Thank you so much," I said. "I mean, thank you very much."

I began to get a little emotional. It was as if "thank you" wasn't enough. It didn't begin to express the gratitude that I felt at the moment. Maybe I should have said, "Thank you, thank you, infinity"?

How do we thank God for the wonders he has done for us? For his love, his forgiveness, his generosity?

The Eucharist—we participate in the Eucharist. The word itself means "thanksgiving." When we gather for Mass, we are invited to enter into Christ's eternal thank you to the Father. It is the perfect, totally adequate thank you.

Finally our hearts can be satisfied. Nothing more can be said; nothing more can be done. For all has been done. What could we possibly add to Jesus's self-gift to the Father?

So we enter into the liturgy and experience Christ and his glory. And to that we simply respond, "Thank you—a lot."

CHAPTER FOURTEEN

Love's Response
• *Fr. Dave* •

As he was setting out on a journey, a man ran up, knelt down
before him, and asked him, "Good teacher, what must I do
to inherit eternal life?" Jesus answered him, "Why do you
call me good? No one is good but God alone. You know the
commandments: 'You shall not kill; you shall not commit
adultery; you shall not steal; you shall not bear false witness;
you shall not defraud; honor your father and your mother.'"
He replied and said to him, "Teacher, all of these I have
observed from my youth." Jesus, looking at him, loved him
and said to him, "You are lacking in one thing. Go, sell what
you have, and give to [the] poor and you will have treasure
in heaven; then come, follow me." At that statement his face
fell, and he went away sad, for he had many possessions."
(Mark 10:17–22)

What now? What does the rich man do now? I mean, he laid the
situation out there for everyone to hear. He had one simple question:
"What must I do to inherit eternal life?"

For me this is one of the most striking stories in all of Scripture.
The young man was stripped, bare, vulnerable. What was he to do?

Imagine the scene for a moment. Jesus had been in the town of Jericho for a number of days and was preparing to leave. At this time Jesus was quite famous, and everyone in the village would have been aware that he was there. The rich man ran up to him. He had to talk to Jesus before he left. He threw himself at Jesus's feet.

The rich man was surely known to the locals. What a sight it must have been to see him running in his costly garments and throwing himself at the feet of a poor man. This in itself is a beautiful image.

And then the young man asks a question. Some questions are of relatively little importance: "Do you want fries with that?" But the question the man had for Jesus has eternal consequences. It is a question that everyone needs to ask. "What must I do to inherit eternal life?"

Did this man realize the import of the question? Would his encounter with Jesus change his life?

Jesus went through a list of things the man should not do.

"You shall not kill."

"Good, because I haven't."

"You shall not commit adultery."

"Nope, haven't done that."

"You shall not steal."

"Three for three. Perhaps this is going to be easier than I thought."

"You shall not bear false witness."

"Never! I would not do that."

"You shall not defraud."

"I'm on a roll."

"Honor your father and mother."

"Of course.

"Jesus, I have obeyed since I was little. I don't do any of those bad things. Lots of people around me did, but I never did any of them."

Jesus then looked upon the man with love: "You are lacking one thing..."

Surely, those in the crowd were all ears. They must have wondered, "What more could a person do?" They would have seen the man's wealth as a sign of God's blessing. They were probably impressed that he had led such a virtuous life, never breaking any of the commandments. What possibly could be lacking?

"Sell all that you have and give to the poor; then come and follow me."

The man's face fell. He simply could not do what Jesus was asking. How sad. What started with such promise and excitement, the rich man running to Jesus and kneeling before him, ended tragically.

This is one of the few stories in which Jesus made a personal invitation to someone and the person said no. There is much to be learned from this encounter. How is it that what started off so wonderfully ended up so terribly wrong? And perhaps more importantly, could that happen to me? To you?

What Now?

We've discussed the fact that our encounters with God are graced moments and that life is ripe with opportunities to encounter the Lord. But these encounters are only the beginning. They hold the possibility of being transformative events in our lives. However, as we see in the story of the rich man, the possibility of something beautiful is not a guarantee.

The rich man had an extraordinary encounter with Jesus. He wanted eternal life. But he loved his possessions more than God. Rather than a moving story of a man giving up everything in order to follow Jesus, we have the tragic account of a dejected man walking away from his Savior—literally walking away from eternal life.

I chose this story for the final encounter for two main reasons. The first is to point out that authentic encounters with the Lord ask something of us. The second is to probe the importance of answering the question, "What must we do to inherit eternal life?"

Encounters with the living God invite us to something new. At times the appropriate response is as simple as a thank you. I think of the ten lepers who were healed, and only one of them returned to thank Jesus. Jesus addressed the leper, "Ten were cleansed, were they not? Where are the other nine?" Then he said to the one who had returned to give thanks, "Stand up and go; your faith has saved you" (Luke 17:17, 19).

Jesus commended this man for his faith. Was only the one who returned to say thank you moved by faith?

I recall hearing that a saint is the one who says thank you and knows who it is that needs to be thanked. Let's not underestimate the beauty in a heart filled with gratitude as well as the emptiness of the heart lacking gratitude. There is grace and power in saying thank you to the Lord for who he is and for what he has done in our lives. We ought to never forget to thank the Lord.

The Lord may ask something else of us: He may invite us to live our lives differently. You see, having an encounter with Christ should change us. Journeying from little or no faith to a personal relationship with Christ should cause a shift in the way we live. We can't be the same.

If we're experiencing God's love, we should become more loving. Knowing his mercy should cause us to be more forgiving, and his patience toward us ought to produce greater patience in us. The Lord's gentleness should give rise to our being gentler. We simply can't receive the grace of God in vain; we need to be changed, converted, and transformed.

This change in us needs to be visible. Others need to not only hear what God has done in us but also see it in the way we live our lives. St. John reminds us that we can't say we love God and hate our brother (see 1 John 4:20). Our love of God and the work he has done in our lives must be visible to a world that desperately needs to see such things. The world is terribly cynical of God's transforming power; we must give witness to this power by showing what God has done in us and for us.

Of course, our change will take time, but it will come if we persevere. At first we may want to change everything all at once, and we can get frustrated that transformation seems to be going slowly. But we can't change everything overnight. Multitasking is not a good approach to the spiritual life.

It is generally more effective to choose one or two things and be intentional in working on those. If impatience is your downfall, then for one year focus on that. I am quite certain that at the end of the year you will be more patient.

When we change in one area of our lives, that change has an impact on other parts of our lives. So your focus on one particular area will have a broader reach. You may be surprised.

Relax. Build slowly and lay solid foundations.

What Must You Do?

The rich man took a step in faith when he approached Jesus. In front of the local townspeople, he asked what he had to do to inherit eternal life. I am sure some people cringed when he asked that question. "Doesn't he know that it is better not to ask questions like that? Isn't it better to stay ignorant? Then we can't be held accountable. Ignorance is bliss, right?"

Of course not. The young man was compelled to ask; he had to know.

So then, what must you do to inherit eternal life? Have you asked? Do you know?

We all need to know the answer to this question. We can't wander aimlessly. Our God is not distant, nor is he indifferent toward us. On the contrary, God desires to be active in our lives. He has a specific will for each of us.

Of course, we need to follow the commandments, as did the rich man. We need to be holy. But what else? What is the Lord asking of you? What is he asking that causes you to pause, to question whether or not you are able or willing to respond?

Rachel was a young woman who loved God with all of her heart. I first met her when she was about sixteen and a sophomore in high school. She was different from most teens in that she was fully and radically committed to the Lord. While some young people love youth group, Rachel loved Christ.

Rachel started college but quickly discerned that it was not for her. "What I really want to do is be a missionary. I want to tell people about the love of God. While some people need a degree for that, I don't think I do." So she left college and became a missionary. She wasn't sure how long she would do this, because she also wanted to eventually get married and raise a family.

I was in touch with Rachel on a regular basis, and I watched her missionary work go from six months to a year, then another and another. People would often ask Rachel how long she was going to do missionary work. Some asked, "When will you get a job?"

Rachel loved what she was doing but began to wonder if she was ever going to find the person with whom she could share her life. She still longed to be married and have children, and the mission work made it difficult to meet and develop a relationship with a potential spouse. Each year she would pray, "What must I do?" She would specifically ask God whether or not he wanted her to do another year of mission work.

Rachel began to feel torn. Yes, she wanted to do whatever the Lord asked, but it seemed that what he was asking was leading her away from marriage and family. At times she experienced a great loneliness. But she continued to seek God, and every time she said yes to another year of mission, it was her total surrender to the Lord. Year after year she went wherever the Lord called: Mexico, Europe, Haiti, the Philippines, and other places. She knew the Lord was faithful. Saying yes to him was of greatest importance to her.

After years of missions the Lord called Rachel to a brief ten-day trip to Africa. As grace would have it, she met another missionary there named Mark. They both got more than they expected from this mission trip. Rachel and Mark are now married with two beautiful children. They continue to work as missionaries, now asking the Lord, "What must we do?"

I am certain that the Lord is not going to ask everyone to leave his or her home and go to the other side of the world in order to share the faith. But what is important is that you grow accustomed to asking the Lord the question, "What must I do?" This isn't a question I ask only once; rather I have asked it many, many times. "Lord, what do I need to do today? What must I do in this situation?"

The Lord wants to be active in our lives. He wants to direct us; he has specific things he wants of us. What's important is that we continually ask the question and wait for a response.

It's All about Jesus

It's always been about Jesus. He broke into human history, and humanity has never been the same.

Jesus also broke into my life, and I have been changed. He did this when I was a young boy and again when I was a teen, then a young adult, then…well, you get the point. The Lord has frequently revealed himself to me and continues to do so. At times I am open to receiving and hearing; and honestly, at times I struggle with being able to hear or respond. But I don't give up; I pray, and I never give up. I pray for the grace to keep going, to not quit, to persevere. The only way I can lose the Lord's prize is by quitting.

The Lord is faithful and true to his word. If I continue to seek him and strive to love and forgive as he did, one day I will be with the Lord in the halls of heaven. If each day I work to be more conformed to Christ and aim to make him known, I will inherit eternal life.

Recall what the rich man wanted: He asked Jesus what he must do to inherit eternal life. Eternal life is the desire of our hearts. Jesus's life, death, and resurrection made eternal life with the Father possible. In order to receive this gift from the Lord, we must live our lives for him.

St. Paul put it beautifully when writing to the Galatians: "I died to the law, that I might live for God. I have been crucified with Christ; yet I live, no longer I, but Christ lives in me; insofar as I now live in the flesh, I live by faith in the Son of God who has loved me and given himself up for me" (Galatians 2:19–20).

What must we do to inherit eternal life? We must believe that Christ lives in us. He is alive in me and in you. Accept the Lord's personal invitation to stop living for yourself, and live your life for a greater purpose. Live your life with an active, vibrant faith in the Son of God, Jesus Christ our Lord—a faith that believes in God's unconditional love and mercy for us as revealed in Jesus's death on the cross; a faith that is visible; a faith that draws people into personal encounters with the life-giving God.

This is my faith, it is yours, and it is the faith of the Church.

Welcome.

Now go tell someone.

1. Pope Francis, homily, December 2, 2013, as quoted by Rome Reports, http://www.romereports.com/pg154927-pope-s-mass-we-must-prepare-for-christmas-it-s-an-encounter-not-just-a-memory--en.

2. Pope Francis, Apostolic Exhortation *Evangelii Gaudium* of the Holy Father Francis to the Bishops, Clergy, Consecrated Persons and the Lay Faithful on the Proclamation of the Gospel in Today's World, 1, 3, http://www.vatican.va/holy_father/francesco/apost_exhortations/documents/papa-francesco_esortazione-ap_20131124_evangelii-gaudium_en.html.

3. Fulton Sheen, radio address, January 21, 1945.

4. Adolphe Adam, "O Holy Night," 1847, http://www.hymnsandcarolsofchristmas.com/Hymns_and_Carols/o_holy_night.htm.

5. St. Jerome, *Commentariorum in Isaiam*, as quoted by Pope Paul VI in "*Dei Verbum*, Dogmatic Constitution on Divine Revelation," November 18, 1965, 25. http://www.vatican.va/archive/hist_councils/ii_vatican_council/documents/vat-ii_const_19651118_dei-verbum_en.html.

6. Mieczyslau Koscielniak, as quoted in Bert Ghezzi, *Voices of the Saints* (New York: Doubleday, 2000), p. 521.

7. US Conference of Catholic Bishops, "Twenty-first Sunday in Ordinary Time," August 25, 2013, http://www.usccb.org/bible/readings/082513.cfm.

8. Pope Paul VI, *Sacrosanctum Concilium*, Constitution on the Sacred Liturgy, 7, December 4, 1963, http://www.vatican.va/archive/hist_councils/ii_vatican_council/documents/vat-ii_const_19631204_sacrosanctum-concilium_en.html.

9. See C.S. Lewis, *The Weight of Glory* (San Francisco: Harper Collins, 2001), p. 45.

ABOUT THE AUTHORS

FR. DAVE PIVONKA, T.O.R., speaks at youth conferences throughout North America. He is the director of Franciscan Pathways, an evangelistic preaching outreach of his Franciscan community. He is the author of *Hiking the Camino: 500 Miles with Jesus.*

DEACON RALPH POYO is the founder of New Evangelization Ministries, which assists pastors in training their parish leadership in evangelization. A popular national speaker, he travels extensively around the United States.